Łukasz Jasiński is a world expert both on Austrian Economics and on Private and Public Health Systems. With this third book he culminates a trilogy dedicated to the much needed analysis of the intellectual, practical and moral shortcomings of Public Health Systems, with special reference to the interventionism on the Health System of the United States before and after the ObamaCare. We find in Dr Jasiński's Austrian Economics analysis a detailed and real life explanation on how one of the much praised elements of the so called Welfare State, the Public Health System, is not only dysfunctional and ill of interventionism but how it could very much improve in terms of cost, efficiency and results through the entrepreneurial creativity and spontaneous coordination of the free market system. With his effort to study urgent and real life problems with the Austrian School of Economics tool kit analysis, Jasiński has become a true model for young Austrian Scholars. Congratulations!

- **Jesús Huerta de Soto**, *Professor of Political Economy, King Juan Carlos University (Madrid, Spain)*

Most Americans do not understand why the health care system is in a deplorable state of disrepair. As Dr. Jasinski notes, many wrongly believe the American health care system is market-based because health insurance is not compulsory in the U.S. Yet state and federal governments have their fingers firmly wrapped around coverage and care decisions, starting with Medicare and Medicaid. Failure to see government intervention and intrusion as the root of the problem has the public searching in all the wrong places for solutions. This book looks squarely at the root of the problem with hope that true free-market solutions can be employed to prevent the American health care system from sliding into a single-payer "solution" that puts government in charge and patients in harm's way.

- **Twila Brase**, *RN, PHN, Co-founder and President of Citizens' Council for Health Freedom (CCHF)*

I0894633

Health Insurance in the United States of America

The U.S. health care system is dominated by private and public (governmental) insurance which makes it difficult for many Americans to imagine access to health care without it. The health care system in the USA is sometimes mistakenly referred to as market-based, partly because of the previous lack of compulsory insurance.

As this book shows, however, even before ObamaCare it was a system heavily influenced by the government. This short and accessible book demonstrates that governmental long-term interventionism in the American health insurance market has led to many contemporary serious problems, such as significant and uncontrolled increases in health care costs, rising health insurance prices, marginalization of direct payments, limited competition, and problems with uninsured Americans. Many observers wrongly blame the market for this state of affairs and demand more regulation, which further deteriorates the situation. The study is divided into two parts: an analysis of the history of interventions (and their effects) in the private health insurance market, and an analysis of the genesis and evolution of governmental Medicare and Medicaid insurance. Thus, the book constitutes a unique synthesis of Austrian theory of interventionism and the history of health insurance in the USA.

This book is vital reading for health economists, managers, and policymakers, as well as those interested in the Austrian approach to economics.

Łukasz Jasiński is an assistant professor employed at the Faculty of Economics of the Maria Curie-Sklodowska University in Lublin (Poland).

Routledge Focus on Economics and Finance

The fields of economics are constantly expanding and evolving. This growth presents challenges for readers trying to keep up with the latest important insights. Routledge Focus on Economics and Finance presents short books on the latest big topics, linking in with the most cutting-edge economics research.

Individually, each title in the series provides coverage of a key academic topic, whilst collectively the series forms a comprehensive collection across the whole spectrum of economics.

The Chief Financial Officer and Corporate Performance
Finance, Governance and Risk
Elżbieta Bukalska, Anna Wawryszuk-Misztal and Tomasz Sosnowski

Artists Labour Market, Cultural Policy and Creative Economy
A Triangular Model in Poland
Dorota Ilczuk, Anna Karpińska, Emilia Cholewicka

Reading John Maynard Keynes
A Short Introduction
Andrés Solimano

Regional Economic Integration in East Asia
Institutions, Agreements and the European Experience
Magdalena Suska

Capital Structure and Firm Performance
Global Financing Decisions among Listed Companies
Ewelina Sokołowska and Milad Zargartalebi

Health Insurance in the United States of America
Austrian Perspectives on Interventionism before ObamaCare
Łukasz Jasiński

For more information about this series, please visit: www.routledge.com/Routledge-Focus-on-Economics-and-Finance/book-series/RFEF

Health Insurance in the United States of America

Austrian Perspectives on Interventionism before ObamaCare

Łukasz Jasiński

Routledge
Taylor & Francis Group
LONDON AND NEW YORK

First published 2025
by Routledge
4 Park Square, Milton Park, Abingdon, Oxon OX14 4RN

and by Routledge
605 Third Avenue, New York, NY 10158

Routledge is an imprint of the Taylor & Francis Group, an informa business

British Library Cataloguing-in-Publication Data
A catalogue record for this book is available from the British Library

ISBN: 978-1-032-96120-0 (hbk)
ISBN: 978-1-032-96124-8 (pbk)
ISBN: 978-1-003-58810-8 (ebk)

DOI: 10.4324/9781003588108

Typeset in Times New Roman
by SPi Technologies India Pvt Ltd (Straive)

To Professor Witold Kwaśnicki, thanks to whom my great adventure with the Austrian School of Economics became possible.

Contents

Figures

Tables

About the author

Łukasz Jasiński is an assistant professor employed at the Faculty of Economics of the Maria Curie-Sklodowska University in Lublin (Poland).

In 2021, he completed his doctoral dissertation entitled *Market processes and interventionism in the health system of the United States of America from the view of the austrian school of economics*. He is also an economist at the Mises Institute of Economic Education (Poland, Wroclaw).

In 2022, on the basis of the decision of the Polish Academy of Sciences (Lublin branch), his book, entitled *Markets vs Public Health Systems: Perspectives from the Austrian School of Economics*, was selected for the best research work for 2021 (Humanities and Social Sciences).

In 2024, Dr Jasiński was awarded a Kosciuszko Foundation grant under the "Exchange Program to the US." The title of the project is "Medical Savings Account and improved access to medical services." Also in the same year, the author of this publication was awarded a scholarship from the Polish Ministry of Science and Higher Education for outstanding young scientists.

Introduction

Sound economic knowledge is indispensable in the study of economic history. Without this knowledge, the interpretation of the socio-economic processes of the past and the conclusions drawn from it may turn out to be incomplete or even wrong. This may lead, for example, to the adoption of inappropriate economic policies.

This issue also concerns the health care system of the USA. From the very beginning of its existence, this system has been subject to constant transformations, more intense or less. These changes have been determined by two main factors: market processes and interventionism. Establishing the essence of the relationship between them and the effects they have been prompting is one of the main purposes of this book.

The main aim of the book is to demonstrate that there are no pure market institutions in the health care system of the USA, and that the influence of the state is constantly growing. This system is part of the so-called hampered economy, where many interventions affect market processes. There are numerous misconceptions about the American system, especially regarding its market nature. In part, this is due to the lack of compulsory health insurance or the significant popularity of private insurance. The permanent problems faced by this system, including a significant increase in the cost and expenditure on medical services or a relatively high percentage of uninsured people, mean that from time to time the idea of creating a single-payer system, i.e., covering all Americans with government health insurance, comes up again. This is supposed to be a response to the alleged market failures in this area.

This study, based mainly on the achievements of the Austrian School, is intellectually opposed to these proposals and indicates that the real cause of the above-mentioned problems is government intervention restricting free market processes. They have a long history and cover many areas of the American system: the health insurance market, the process of educating doctors, hospitals, government insurance for the elderly and the poor, and regulations covering the marketing of drugs. Their ultimate

DOI: 10.4324/9781003588108-1

consequence is a non-market stimulation of demand for medical services while limiting their supply (and competition).

From an economic point of view, it is essential to know how the system of interventionism functions in the indicated area, and whether it allows to achieve the goals set by its promoters, especially when it comes to the availability of medical goods and services.

The causes of the current problems of the American health care system must be sought in the past: what the key interventions were and how they have affected the current situation. To this end, I have analysed data from the period stretching from the turn of the 19th and 20th centuries to 2013, the last year before the Patient Protection and Affordable Care Act (PPACA, more commonly known as "ObamaCare").

In this book, the history of individual interventions in the indicated areas is covered – both on the demand side (private and public insurance) and on the supply side (doctors, hospitals, and medicines). The legitimacy of their introduction and the effects they brought have been thoroughly analysed. Numerous references to market-based solutions that functioned to a limited extent against the background of these interventions have been considered. Several passages also draw attention to the dynamic nature of interventionism.

It is particularly significant to analyse the private health insurance and hospital markets. One in two Americans has private health insurance, but decades of government regulation of the market, both at the federal and state levels, have significantly skewed it, which has contributed to a significant increase in insurers' spending, insurance premiums, and problems for employers and the insured. Nowadays, it is impossible to offer real health insurance in the USA. Private health insurance itself is increasingly reminiscent of social insurance. On the other hand, the American hospital system is negatively distinguished by the highest dynamics of cost growth, which results from several monopoly privileges restricting competition. In most states, there are still laws that significantly restrict the construction of new (competitive) facilities. As a result, many hospitals can artificially inflate the prices of their services, as they do not have to fear any competition.

These are not the only problems of the American health care system. In fact, it is very complex and consists of numerous institutions responsible for organizing and financing access to medical services. Therefore, in this book, its key elements and evolution have been meticulously described, which is to allow a better understanding of the specifics of the issues discussed.

1 Evolution of private health insurance

The beginnings of private health insurance and competition with Blue Cross and Blue Shield plans

To fully understand the current shape and problems of the American health care system, it is essential to analyse the emergence and development of the private health insurance market. Today, health insurance plays a key role in this system. However, this is not the result of unfettered market processes but rather of successive government interventions at both the federal and state levels. Insurance is often treated as the only rational market option for financing access to medical goods and services. An expensive alternative is direct payments. Importantly, however, the role of private health insurance, because of many government interventions in the past, has been to some extent exaggerated, to the detriment of other market solutions and insurance itself. Today, nearly one in two Americans (either as an employee or family member) has access to medical services through private employer-provided insurance, whose cost is also steadily increasing. This means that in the market's efforts to reduce spending (or the rate of its growth) allocated to health care, it is necessary to consider not only government health programmes but also the private health insurance market (Kaiser Family Foundation, 2011).

Although it may seem unlikely to contemporary Americans, at the turn of the 20th century private health insurance played a marginal role in the American health care system. However, these were completely different realities due to the level of medicine and technology. At the beginning of the 20th century, the biggest problem was not, as it is today, high bills for medical services, but lost income caused by an employee's illness or accident. The situation was even more difficult if the employee in question was the main breadwinner for his family. Melissa Thomasson of the University of Miami cites as an example a 1919 study conducted in Illinois showing that lost wages due to a worker's illness were four times higher than medical expenses related to the treatment of the disease. Paying for health insurance was, therefore, pointless. Instead, sickness

DOI: 10.4324/9781003588108-2

insurance, which covers lost income or part of it at the time of illness, was more popular (Thomasson, 2003).

This type of lack of insurance was, therefore, not the result of lack of access to information, knowledge, or ignorance of employees, but rather a deliberate action resulting from economic (financial) calculation. Progress in medicine at the turn of the 19th and 20th centuries was just beginning to gain momentum, and medicine itself began to play an increasingly important role in the treatment process which began to move from homes to hospitals or doctors' offices. Not without significance was also the emergence of government licenses for doctors or hospitals. Society began to view medicine differently and to place more in it than just a belief in providing them with treatment. There was also a growing belief in the greater effectiveness of treatment methods or drugs (Thomasson, 2003; Rosenberg 1987).

On the one hand, the increase in demand (to a lesser extent) and on the other hand, the artificial limitations on the supply of doctors or hospitals (to a greater extent) contributed to the increase in the cost of health care in the USA at the beginning of the 20th century. These phenomena occurred along with the emergence of new discoveries and technologies in medicine, which ultimately led to the belief that the technology itself was responsible for the increase in costs. These were also the conclusions of the 1925 Committee on the Cost of Medical Care which investigates the causes of cost increases. However, in fact, the main reason for this situation was the licensing of doctors or hospitals, imposed on them by government-backed institutions, such as the American Medical Association.

An increase in demand alone, without permanent constraints on the supply side, could not have contributed to an increase in costs. This is primarily because every consumer has limited financial resources and will think seriously before spending them on a particular good or service. Secondly, at that time, the market for financing medical services was not yet dominated by third-party payers, so the consumer was more price-sensitive than today. Thirdly, the natural reaction of the unfettered market to the growing demand is to offer products that are more qualitative and cheaper than the ones offered by the competition. If a new, technologically advanced product appears in each market and is gaining more and more interest among consumers, then competitors wishing to enter this market must offer at least a product of similar quality, but at a lower price (an additional advantage of the leader is having been the first to innovate and gain trust). And fourthly, in the case of a new and advanced good or service, it is difficult to talk about an increase in prices, because it is a unique product that has not had its counterparts in the past.

In addition, the role of the entrepreneur is to meet the needs of consumers. If consumers believe that such products benefit them, they buy them at an even higher price because they believe that it improves their situation.

However, market processes do not lead to the introduction of more and more expensive goods or services purchased by increasingly desperate consumers. On the contrary, as Thomas DiLorenzo (2004, p. 120–122) points out, there have been many such cases in the history of the U.S. economy:

> In the 1920s it took 79 hours of work to buy a nice men's suit; today it takes less than half that. At the beginning of the twentieth century the average American family spent three-quarters of its income on food, clothing, and shelter; today it spends about one-third on those items, and spends an even greater proportion on taxes.
>
> In 1908 the typical American worker had to work two years to earn enough money to buy an average-quality car. Today a Ford Taurus costs an American worker about eight months of labour, but the car is a technological miracle compared with the cars of yesteryear, with standard air conditioning, power seats, safety devices of all kinds, cruise control, a sunroof, tinted glass, a CD player, and so on. In 1970 an IBM mainframe computer sold for around $4.7 million; today, a personal computer that operates thirteen times faster goes for under $1,000.

Thus, the notion that technology leads to an increase in the cost of medical goods and services in the USA has its roots in events that occurred about 100 years ago and earlier. It is also worth noting that while in the 1920s supply-side factors were behind the increase in costs, after World War II demand factors played a greater role, with third-party payers at the forefront (Blue Cross, Blue Shield, commercial health insurance, Medicare, and Medicaid). The old realities also influenced the debate on the introduction of universal (public) health insurance. In the 1920s, there was debate over the introduction of health insurance that was more like sickness insurance or disability insurance. In the 1930s, on the other hand, there were propositions that health insurance finance access to hospital services, etc.

However, the lack of adequate health technology was not the only reason for the marginal contribution of private health insurance in financing Americans' access to medical services in the early 20th century. Another problem was the *actuarial barrier* of sorts. Insurance companies were concerned about the phenomenon of negative selection and moral hazard. Insurance companies did not have sufficient information about the health of potential insured persons, which limited their ability to estimate appropriate premiums adequate to the risk represented. Therefore, it can be concluded that health as an insured subject was uninsurable at that time. Interestingly, the solution resulting in the dynamic development of private health insurance in the first half of the 20th century did not come from the insurance companies themselves but had its roots in the solutions used by Blue Cross and Blue Shield. In the 1930s, these institutions began to offer their own health plans based on prepaid health care. Their way of functioning was, therefore, much closer to modern medical networks offering subscriptions than to the activities of insurance companies using actuarial methods to calculate insurance risk. From the perspective of the insurance industry, it was crucial for these institutions to find a simple and effective way to reduce the problem of moral hazard. That solution was to focus its business operations on offering health plans only to groups of employees (Thomasson, 2003).

Moral hazard is a deliberate action that leads to an increase in the benefits achieved by the beneficiary who is not burdened with additional costs in this respect. In the case of health insurance, it may be the payment of a lower premium by ill people who have withheld information about their health from the insurer. This further leads to inflated losses for insurers, which may result in the destabilization of the entire insurance programme. Although it is not unusual today to offer health insurance to groups of workers, about a century ago it was both simple and innovative. Taking up a job in a company was obviously aimed at obtaining an adequate income and not health insurance, as may have been the case with individuals wishing to insure themselves individually. Thus, in the case of workers' insurance, the problem of moral hazard was no longer an insurmountable barrier.

Ultimately, the success of Blue Cross and Blue Shield with their own health plans, and the continued promising growth prospects of this market, prompted insurance companies to act. Although insurers were not the first to enter this market, their expansion was rapid and in a very short time, they became the main institutional competitor to the Blue Cross/Blue Shield plans. While in the 1940s there were more participants enrolled in Blue Cross/Blue Shield plans, at the beginning of the next decade the situation changed in favour of insurance companies. For instance, according to statistics, in 1940 just over 6 million people were covered by hospital services in Blue Cross/Blue Shield plans, compared to 3.7 million people with group and individual health insurance. On the other hand, in 1955, despite a significant increase in the number of participants in Blue Cross/Blue Shield plans to almost 49 million (an increase of over 700%), private health insurance was already more popular, covering more than 57 million people (an increase of almost 1,500%) (Reed & Carr, 1969, p. 9). Similar estimates are quoted by the Health Insurance Institute (1966, p. 14), according to which in 1951 41.5 million people were covered by group or individual hospital insurance offered by commercial insurance companies and only 40.9 million people were covered by the Blue Cross and Blue Shield plans. See Figures 1.1 and 1.2 for details.

The presented data also shows that insurers had more participants enrolled in plans offering surgical services from the beginning of the

Figure 1.1 Number of health plan beneficiaries – 1940–1967.

Source: Own study based on: Reed & Carr, 1969, p. 9; Reed, 1967, p. 12.

Note: In addition to the Blue Cross/Blue Shield offer and insurers, health plans include various types of independent plans, such as plans of consumer communities, employers' and staff associations, medical communities or private group clinics. Their share, however, was marginal: in 1967, the number of beneficiaries eligible for hospital services amounted to just over 7 million (4% of all beneficiaries), and 8.5 million (5% of all beneficiaries) for surgical services.

For better clarity of the results, the values given for participants enrolled in insurers' plans are not duplicated. During a given year, participants could be enrolled in, for example, individual insurance, and then, after finding a new job, they could join the employment insurance.

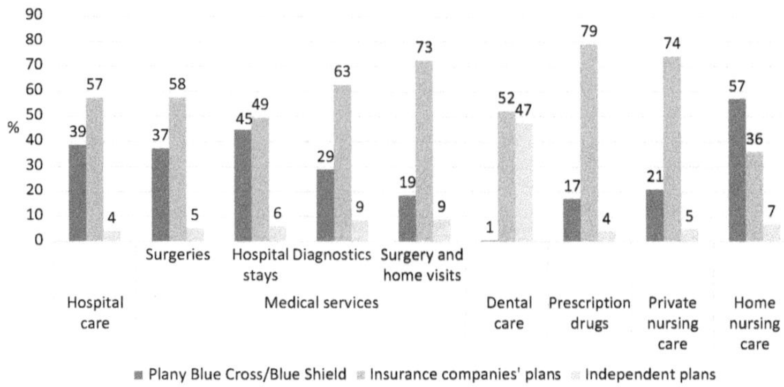

Figure 1.2 Share of all beneficiaries (in percentage) with access to individual benefits in the plans.

Source: own study based on: Reed & Carr, 1969, p. 7.

competition. Their advantage also in hospital services resulted from, among other things, differences in the functioning of these institutions. Insurance companies were for-profit institutions, and the commercial nature of their activities proved to be an important factor in gaining this advantage. Unlike private insurers, Blue Cross and Blue Shield were non-profit institutions, which, as discussed in the previous section, gave them several important benefits, including tax benefits. However, these benefits also came at a price in the form of their commitment to apply uniform risk assessment criteria (community rating) to all participants in the programme.

The lack of price discrimination may have been less noticeable in groups in which, for example, older people were a significant proportion, and there were fewer younger and potentially less satisfied people. On the other hand, if, for example, Blue Cross approached a large company employing mostly relatively young and healthy employees, the insurance company's competitive offer was more attractive to the employer and employees precisely because of the possibility of differentiating premiums for individual groups of employees. Of course, insurance companies were able to capitalize on this gap and offer more competitively priced insurance, as actuarial risk calculation was (and still is) at the core of their business. Therefore, the unfettered activity of insurers led to a decrease in prices in relation to the offer of competitors.

Interestingly, there was even a situation in which Blue Cross and Blue Shield, to remain competitive, even began to abandon the use of community rating, thus losing government support. They were forced to do so by their status as a non-profit organization and the growing problems with elderly patients generating higher and higher costs for hospitals. Meanwhile, private insurers using risk-based calculation had no such problems (Jeurissen, 2010, p. 47).

These phenomena illustrate well how the development of insurance has contributed to improving access to medical goods and services for millions of Americans. At this point, it is also necessary to emphasise another critical issue. Health insurance, especially in its group (employee) form, is more popular in urban and more industrialized areas than in smaller towns. Therefore, one can get the impression that the insurance market is not functioning properly. Similar arguments can be raised, e.g., in the matter of obtaining better insurance conditions for younger people, etc (Congressional Budget Office, 1994, p. 5). The problem with these types of allegations, however, is that their supposed accuracy is really based on the normative assumption that everyone should have access to insurance, pay the same, fair premium, etc. Both theory and experience show that the benefits resulting from the development of private health insurance are a kind of bonus that relieves a part of the society from incurring higher costs because of the occurrence of undesirable events in the future, such as illness. There are many conditions influencing the shape of the unfettered health insurance market which give the possibility of covering a larger or smaller part of the society with such insurance.[1] Indeed, in this sector of the economy direct payments also play a fundamental (in economic terms) function. Goods and services such as food, clothing and even transport are undoubtedly crucial for maintaining a basic standard of living, and yet access to them is not financed by insurance to the extent that medical goods and services are.

Employee health insurance as an alternative to higher income

U.S. economic history also shows that it was not just technology and competitive processes that were behind the growing number of Americans with a specific health plan. Government regulations also had a significant impact on the growing popularity of these plans. As it turns out, the USA joining the war effort during World War II had far-reaching implications for the health insurance market as well. The economy, in addition to shifting the structure of production to warfare, was also subject to other regulations, including price controls which, in this case, meant setting maximum prices for many goods and services. Such solutions are often used by states in various specific situations. It is worth noting that in the event of a country entering a war, an increase in the price of basic goods is not unusual. Prices are rising, among other things, due to growing anxiety and the consequent increase in demand, an increase in military production at the expense of basic goods and services, and the conscription of men and women of working age. That is why the governments of the countries involved in the war often introduced price controls. However, this did not improve the situation of society, as the lack of incentive in the form of sufficiently high profits had a negative impact on the already limited production of basic goods and led to the development of black markets.

In this case, price controls also extended to the labour market.[2] Employers, because of the reduction in the workforce, began to compete for more qualified employees. This resulted in rising wages which were also subject to control (the wage is ultimately the price that the employer must pay for the services rendered by the employee). As in the case of the control of other prices, such a regulation could not be effective because it did not remove the main cause of rising wages, i.e., the limited supply of labour caused by the war. The needs of employers did not disappear with the introduction of the maximum wage level either. Entrepreneurs, as is often the case, adapted to the situation and, in fact, changed the form of excessive remuneration.[3] Instead of the higher salary, already prohibited by law, non-wage employee benefits in the form of health plans/insurance were offered as *compensation*.

As mentioned earlier, this market had been developing well from the 1930s and gaining more and more customers. Importantly for insurers or Blues Cross/Blue Shield, the premium (or part of it) that was paid by the employer was exempt from income tax, thus employees did not incur additional costs in fully or partially employer-sponsored health plans. This was the result of the assumptions made in the past by the US Internal Revenue Service (IRS). From 1913, the IRS had interpreted health and casualty insurance paid in whole or in part by employers as non-taxable supplemental employee benefits. However, the IRS did not issue a conclusive ruling on the matter until 1943 (when it ruled that benefits not paid in cash should not be taxable). Eventually, the Office's position was strengthened by Congress which in 1954 passed Section 106 of the Internal Revenue Code stipulating that employers' contributions to health and accident insurance were also to be exempt from payroll taxes (Congressional Budget Office, 1994, p. 5).

These new regulations further influenced the growing popularity of private health insurance. However, this was no longer the result of completely unhindered market processes but of the regulations related to the tax law. In addition, some of the contributions paid by employees were deductible from income tax, which in fact reduced the cost of health insurance. However, employees could no longer count on similar tax reliefs in the case of direct expenses for medical services, individual insurance, car insurance (comprehensive insurance) or home insurance. To some extent, therefore, health insurance became an additional tool to reduce the tax burden. Such benefits are only the aftermath of the regulation of prices and wages during the World War II (which demonstrates that once interventions are undertaken in *exceptional* situations, they become a permanent element of the economy).

Further regulations of private health insurers

The above-described factors contributed to a significant increase in the number of Americans insured (especially the ones insured by their employers). According to estimates by the Health Insurance Association of America (1992) (HIAA), in 1940 only 10% of the population had a private (individual or group) health plan, while in 1970 it was already 80%, and in the mid-1970s and early 1980s more than 80% of the population had one. Later, this percentage began to decline due to the number of people retiring, among other things.

While tax regulations influenced the popularity of group health insurance, the insurance market operated on relatively liberal principles. Private insurance companies calculated risk based on statistical data, and the future problems of prepaid health care plans (Blue Cross/Blue Shield) related to ageing beneficiaries and equal premiums were not yet so apparent. Nevertheless, the above conditions pointed to certain scratches which, together with subsequent interventions, led to serious cracks in the seemingly market-oriented, but in fact increasingly interventionist health care system.

Further regulations of insurers turned out to be crucial in this process. Today, the insurance market is regulated by several regulations that have their roots in the Sherman Antitrust Act of the late 19th century which was intended to prevent monopolistic practices. The law enforced the use of the so-called *affordability*. This means that in most states insurers must have their insurance rates approved if they want to sell their products. Previously, insurers had shared data on claims to determine appropriate rates and premiums. If this data was reliable and abundant enough, insurance companies managed their business better, offered better-priced products, and expanded into new markets. For the insurance market, the Sherman Act came into effect in 1944 based on a Supreme Court ruling that insurance is part of interstate commerce and, therefore, the activities of insurance companies should be regulated by Congress. This meant that the data previously used in this market was not to be shared anymore. The legislator feared that with such data the insurer could gain a significant share of the market and impose monopoly prices. The real problem, however, aside from the validity of the Sherman Act,[4] was that the prohibition applied to the core business of insurance companies, and its enforcement would result in a significant restriction of their functioning. Therefore, in 1945, the McCarran–Ferguson Act was introduced, thanks to which insurance companies could continue to use previously developed methods of determining rates and thus premiums for insurance products. However, this was tantamount to granting state authorities additional powers to protect customers from monopolistic practices (Iwanik, 2009). From the government's point of view, interference in the process of setting rates (and, in fact, prices) was a natural consequence of agreeing to maintain the existing, necessary practices of sharing data on claims. Thus, the Sherman and McCarran–Ferguson Acts gave rise to many state-level interventions that extended to health insurance markets and increasingly affected them in the decades that followed.

Indeed, the private health insurance market was increasingly regulated, especially at the state level. These regulations had a significant impact on the activities of insurance companies, thus slowly distorting the essence of concluding such agreements. Here are a few examples presented by Warren Gibson (2018, p. 21):

- It was illegal to offer policies across state lines, which suppressed choices and increased prices, essentially cartelizing health insurance by state.
- Employers were (and still are) given a tax break for providing health insurance (but not auto insurance) to their employees, reducing the incentive for covered employees to economize on health care while driving up prices for individual buyers. People stayed locked in jobs out of fear of losing health policies.
- State regulators forbade policies that excluded certain coverage items, even if policyholders were amenable to such plans.
- Many states made it illegal to price discriminate based on health status.
- The law forbade associated health plans, which would allow organizations like churches or civic groups to pool risk and offer alternatives.
- Medicaid and Medicare made up half of the health care system.

The prohibition of price discrimination based on individual risk factors or the requirement to cover certain insurance benefits caused insurance companies to lose their attributes thanks to which they had maintained a market advantage over Blue Cross and Blue Shield plans. In fact, the differences between the health plans offered by these institutions began to blur, to the detriment of the insured. It also meant an intensification of the adverse phenomena that insurance companies feared so much at the beginning of the 20th century, i.e., negative selection and moral hazard.

Nevertheless, the intensification of those phenomena was the result of state regulations that required, among other things, insuring all applicants regardless of their health condition, as well as the use of uniform risk assessment criteria, the so-called community rating). A natural consequence of this situation was a growing number of behaviours referred to as *free riding*, as these regulations encourage people to remain uninsured when they are healthy and to insure themselves when they are sick, which, in fact, contradicts the point of insurance. Due to rising premiums and too wide coverage, health insurance is becoming less and less attractive for healthy people who rarely get sick, and more and more popular among people with higher health risks. People with lower health risks resign from insurance, which puts even more pressure on premiums to rise and contributes to more cancellations (Goodman, Musgrave & Herrick, 2004, pp. 220–221). This is a short description of the so-called *spiral of affordability*, i.e. a very undesirable phenomenon, ultimately resulting in rising insurance prices along with a decreasing number of the people insured.[5]

Statistics illustrate a significant increase in the number of mandatory benefits to which the insured are entitled. While in 1970 the total number was only 48, in 2008 it rose to over 2000 (Hoppe, 2006). It was partly due to the lobbying of certain social groups to include services that would otherwise be excluded by insurers. Rare but publicized cases of people who were refused to have the costs of heart transplantation covered or to be financed expensive experimental therapies also played a role (Folland, Goodman & Stano, 2013, p. 400). Other examples of regulations common in most states require insurers to finance, among others: the costs of alcoholism treatment, the costs of using the services of chiropractors, podiatrists or psychologists, the costs of drug addiction treatment and such specific services as acupuncture, in vitro fertilization or marriage counselling (Goodman, Musgrave & Herrick, 2004, p. 221). Providers of medical services also sought to include them in the scope of mandatory services. These groups made profits at the expense of the rest of the insured.

The expansion of interventions in the second half of the 20th century was complemented by the Health Insurance Portability and Accountability Act (HIPPA) passed in 1996. From the perspective of health insurance, their main objective was to support employees who may have lost favourable insurance conditions due to a high health risk while changing or losing their jobs. The provisions in the act prohibited insurance companies from excluding employees from insurance because of their health condition. The multitude of requirements set by HIPPA also resulted in an increase in the costs of complying with the provisions of the Act. In addition to insurance companies, also doctors, hospitals and other institutions must comply with these regulations. These entities employ lawyers and other experts to assist them in meeting the requirements of the Act (Folland, Goodman & Stano, 2013, pp. 398–399). This is mainly related to the protection of data concerning patients' health, the course of their disease, etc., which is to increase data security, patients' knowledge of the use of their data or improve the functioning of the entire information management system between individual institutions.[6]

In addition to the high complexity of the regulations, the legitimacy of their introduction remains problematic, as problems related to insurance coverage or, more broadly, access to specific medical services are a consequence of several interventions since the beginning of the 20th century. The problem is also that the HIPPA regulations treat private health insurance as the main form of financing access to medical services, which had not been the norm before.

The conclusion from the history of these interventions is that the tax policy itself, increasing the benefits of having occupational health insurance, was not yet so harmful. It only influenced the market and (to some extent) the competitive process of development of individual forms of insurance and alternative forms of financing access to medical services (insurance at the expense of direct payments). It also had an impact on the formation of a new institutional structure (group employee insurance), which in turn became the subject of further interventions – more restrictive of market processes and thus even more difficult to develop alternative forms of financing access to medical services (especially direct payments), which are so important for maintaining their rational consumption. This is important because consumers (the insured) are less sensitive to the market price. After all, they pay a premium that is only a fraction of the total cost of medical service and, additionally, they reduce the cost of insurance through tax breaks, which further reinforces their sense that such services are free.

Notes

1 Insurance companies have been gradually developing their products through better risk assessment, thanks to which the number of people insured individually, and not only insured by the employer, also increased.
2 Price (and wage) controls were enacted in The Stabilization Act of 1942 of October 3, 1942.
3 It is worth noting that the penalty for failure to comply with the new law was a fine of $1,000, imprisonment for one year, or both at the same time.
4 For more about criticism of the Sherman Act, see: DiLorenzo, T. (1991, pp. 1–6).
5 As it turns out, although the spiral of affordability is now strongly associated with the ObamaCare reform, it was in fact a phenomenon that had occurred even before the reform came into force. However, the previous cases had a different, i.e. less dynamic (in terms of price increases) course than ObamaCare.
6 See: Centers for Disease Control and Prevention, n.d.

References

Centers for Disease Control and Prevention (n.d.). Health Insurance Portability and Accountability Act of 1996 (HIPAA), www.cdc.gov/phlp/php/resources/health-insurance-portability-and-accountability-act-of-1996-hipaa.html?CDC_AAref_Val=https://www.cdc.gov/phlp/publications/topic/hipaa.html (accessed: 19.10.2024).

Congressional Budget Office (1994). *The Tax Treatment of Employment-Based Health Insurance*. Congressional Budget Office.

DiLorenzo, T. (1991). 'The Antitrust Economists' Paradox', *Austrian Economics Newsletter, no number*: 1–6.

DiLorenzo, T. (2004). *How Capitalism Saved America: The Untold History of Our Country, from the Pilgrims to the Present*. Crown Forum. [Ebook].

Folland, S., Goodman, A. C., & Stano, M. (2013). *The Economics of Health and Health Care* (7th ed.). Pearson.

Gibson, W. (2018). Real health insurance is a crime. In Foundation for Economic Education (Ed.), *FEE Guides to Healthcare: Answers to the Health Care Conundrum*, Foundation for Economic Education, pp. 18–22.

Goodman, J. C., Musgrave, G. L., & Herrick D. M. (2004). *Lives at Risk. Single-Payer National Health Insurance around the World*. Rowman & Littlefield Publishers.

Health Insurance Association of America (1992). *1991 Source Book of Health Insurance Data*. Health Insurance Association of America.

Health Insurance Institute (1966). *Source Book of Health Insurance Data, 1965*. Health Insurance Institute.

Hoppe, H. H. (2006). Uncertainty and Its Exigencies: The Critical Role of Insurance in the Free Market, www.mises.org/library/uncertainty-and-its-exigencies-critical-role-insurance-free-market (accessed: 19.10.2024).

Iwanik, J. (2009). The Regulated Insurance Market, www.mises.org/library/regulated-insurance-market (accessed: 18.10.2024).

Jeurissen, P. (2010). *For-Profit Hospitals: A Comparative and Longitudinal Study of the For-Profit hospital sector in four Western countries*. Erasmus University Press.

Kaiser Family Foundation (2011). Pulling It Together: Rising Health Costs Are Not Just a Federal Budget Problem, www.kff.org/health-costs/perspective/pulling-it-together-rising-health-costs-are/ (accessed: 18.10.2024).

Reed, L. S. (1967). 'Private Health Insurance: Coverage and Financial Experience, 1940–66', *Social Security Bulletin, 11*: 12.

Reed, L. S., & Carr, W. (1969), 'Private Health Insurance in the United States, 1967', *Social Security Bulletin, 2*: 7.

Rosenberg, C. E. (1987). *The Care of Strangers: The Rise of America's Hospital System*. Basic Books.

Thomasson, M. (2003). Health Insurance in the United States, http://www.eh.net/encyclopedia/health-insurance-in-the-united-states/ (accessed: 18.10.2024).

2 Private health insurance in the 21st century

Private employee health insurance

The problem of constantly growing group (employee) health insurance premiums is special because this type of insurance in 2018 already covered more than 153 million people aged 0–64, which amounts to about 58% of the US population (Kaiser Family Foundation, n.d.). The increase in premiums applies to both individual[1] and family-insured employees, as shown in Figure 2.1.

It is also particularly important that the dynamics of the increase in health insurance premiums were much higher than the increase in the inflation rate and, more importantly, the earnings of employees.

It is also worth noting that these were not exceptions in the form of multi-year periods, but a steady trend since the Kaiser Family Foundation (KFF)[2] acquired and published this data (Figure 2.2).

By 2013 alone, before ObamaCare came into effect, premiums had increased by 182% (compared to 1999). Additional employee costs (in addition to the part of their premium) in the form of deductible, copayment and coinsurance grew even faster – by 196%. In turn, the inflation rate (CPI) increased by 40% and workers' earnings by 50% (Kaiser Family Foundation, 2018). This is particularly important because, according to a survey conducted in 2018 by KFF, respondents[3] indicated too high a cost of insurance as the main reason for not having insurance (45% of responses). Yet another study (from 2017) conducted among uninsured workers who could have signed up for insurance but had not taken advantage of the offer showed that in 9 out of 10 cases the reason was also its too high a cost (Tolbert et al., 2019).

Other reasons for employees not having insurance include waiting periods (grace periods), part-time or temporary work status, or lack of health insurance offered by the employer.[4] The percentage of all companies offering health insurance to their employees decreased from 66% (1999) to 57% (2019) in companies with fewer than 200 employees (Figure 2.3). Most workers in the USA, however, are employed by large companies[5]

DOI: 10.4324/9781003588108-3

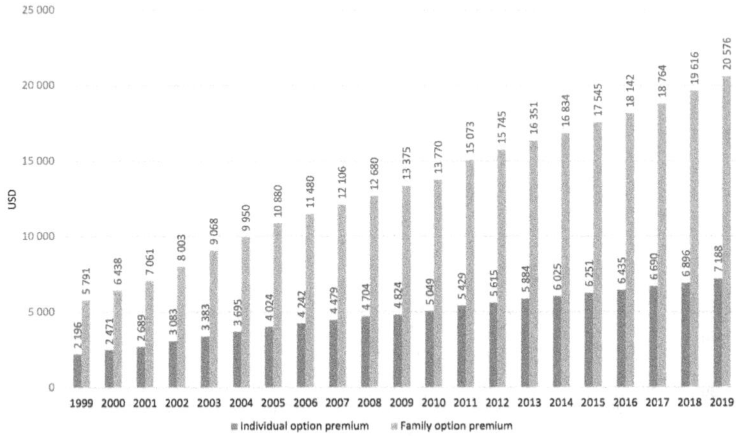

Figure 2.1 Average amount of contributions in occupational health insurance in 1999–2019.

Source: Own study based on: Kaiser Family Foundation, 2019c.

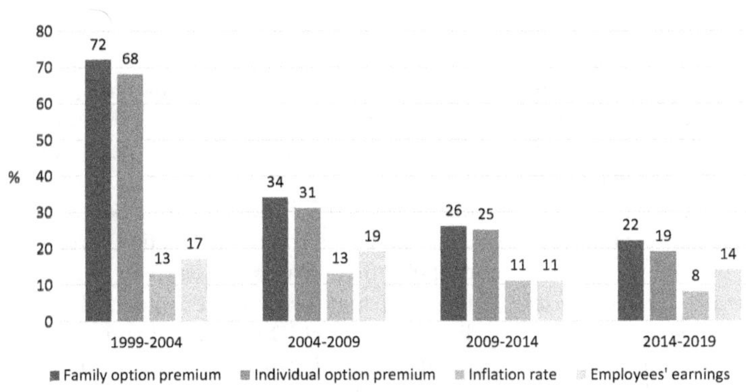

Figure 2.2 Comparison of the growth dynamics (in percentage) of employee health insurance premiums, inflation rate and employee earnings in the years 1999–2019.

Source: Own study based on: Kaiser Family Foundation, 2019a, p. 42; Kaiser Family Foundation, 2019c.

that do offer health insurance. In 2019, 90% of employees were employed by companies that offered health benefits to at least some of their employees. The data also shows that in the same year, about 80% of employees employed by companies offering them health insurance were eligible to join these programmes. 76% of them took advantage of this opportunity,

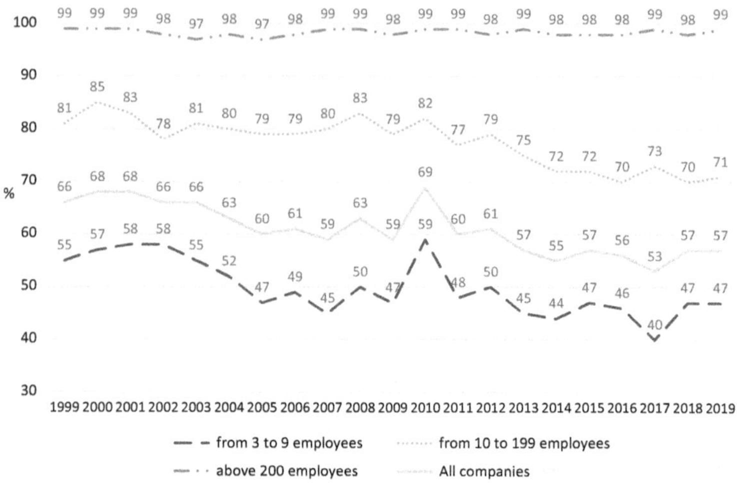

Figure 2.3 Percentage of companies offering health insurance, depending on the number of employees.

Source: Own study based on: Kaiser Family Foundation, 2019a, p. 13.

and thus 61% of all employees in these companies were covered by health insurance.[6] After considering employees of companies that do not offer health insurance, the percentage of people insured in their companies is 55% (Kaiser Family Foundation, 2019a, p. 65, 68).

On this basis, it can be concluded that it is difficult to make everyone insured by means of regulations, and the effects of such actions are different than expected. Other noticeable effects for employees may be growing out-of-pocket expenses. Although it may seem so, it is not a defect of insurance or the effect of a defective market. Direct costs incurred by the insured are an important element of health insurance, as they limit excessive consumption, thus introducing a framework for more rational consumption of health services. Their use significantly affects the stability of health programmes, and thus the certainty of access to medical services needed by the insured. Their complete elimination would further affect the increase in contributions. In the USA, there are several types of direct payments covered by the insured: deductible, copayment and coinsurance. Their special features are presented in Table 2.1.

As in the case of insurance premiums, these costs (apart from copayments) also grew at a faster rate than employees' earnings. The largest increase was recorded in the cost of deductible which increased by 176% between 2006 and 2016. By comparison, the combined cost of all three types of direct payments increased by 54%, and employees' earnings by 29% (Figure 2.4).

Table 2.1 Types of direct payments in health insurance

Types		
Deductible	*Copayment*	*Coinsurance*
The amount that the insured must cover in the first place before the insurance comes into effect.	A predetermined rate that the insured must pay for the use of a given service.	As opposed to copayment, the percentage cost that the insured incurs for the medical bill.
Examples		
A $200 deductible on a $1,000 medical bill means that the insured will pay $200 first, and the insurer will bear its cost ($800) second.	The insured person pays additional fees for these services: $10 for each day of hospital stay, $20 for each visit to the doctor, etc.	Health insurance with a copayment of 18% means that the insured covers 18% of the bill and the insurer covers the other 82%.

Source: Own study based on: Getzen, 2012.

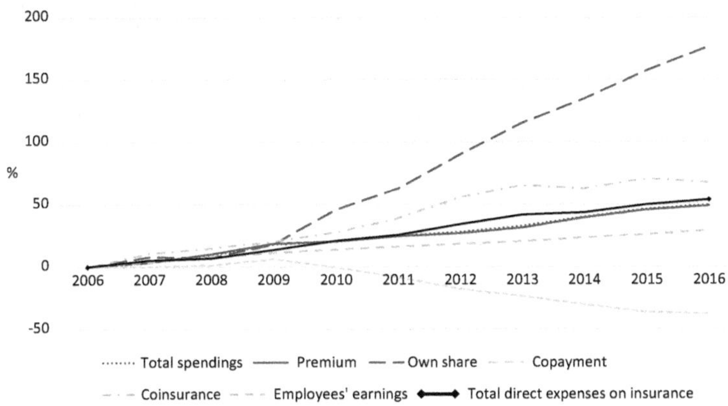

Figure 2.4 Growth rate (in percentage) of individual types of direct payments compared to employees' earnings and the cost of insurance in the years 2006–2016.

Source: Own study based on: G. Claxton et al., 2018.

Note: The survey was conducted in large enterprises, i.e., with more than 200 employees. The data only reflects a breakdown of costs incurred under the benefit plan and does not include balancing payments that beneficiaries may pay to health care providers for out-of-network services or out-of-pocket payments for services not covered by insurance.

The average cost of a deductible was $151 in 2006 and $417 in 2016. The cost of coinsurance also increased: from $149 to $249. In contrast, copayment costs fell from $225 to $140 over the same period.

Total expenses: the sum of premiums and direct expenses for insurance. *Total direct expenses for insurance*: the sum of copayments, deductible, and coinsurance. *Insurance premium*: the total premium that includes the part paid by the employer and the employee.

Yet another study conducted by the KFF demonstrated that the percentage of beneficiaries spending more than $1,000 per year on direct payments (related to insurance) increased from 17.1% in 2005 to 24.2% in 2015. Despite this, 62% of them spent no more than $500 on this type of spending (Figure 2.5).

The amount of the deductible or other costs set in the insurance contract does not mean additional costs for the employee. Some of the insured, for example, do not generate in a given year costs exceeding the established limit of the deductible and thus triggering the liability of the insurance company. While the insured are not enthusiastic about rising direct expenses, insurance covers a large part of their bill. Perhaps the role of the growing direct spending is misunderstood by the Americans accustomed to receiving access to medical services through insurance. On this basis, one should not draw too far-reaching conclusions about the problems of the insurance market but rather about the lack of attractive market alternatives. This shortage, however, does not result from the monopoly of insurance companies but from many interventions creating, in fact, the illusion of free and trouble-free access to medical services through insurance.

Interestingly, the share of individual forms of direct payments has changed over the years. For instance, in 2003, the largest additional cost for family insurance was copayment, and the lowest expenses were related to the coverage of the deductible. After over a decade, these proportions reversed significantly in favour of the deductible – 51% to 19% in 2017 (Figure 2.6).

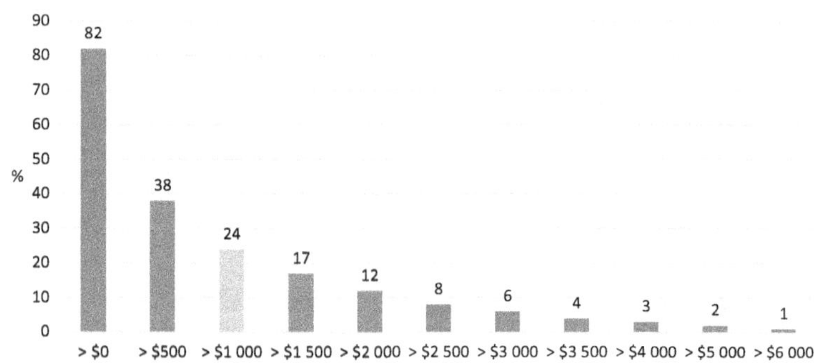

Figure 2.5 Percentage of beneficiaries with certain direct expenditure thresholds in 2015.

Source: Own study based on: Saywer, Cox, & Claxton, 2017.

Note: The majority (99%) of employees are covered with partially or fully restricted annual direct expenditure limits. This limit is referred to as the so-called *out-of-pocket maximum*. This is a result of the requirements imposed by the ObamaCare Act. In 2019, the maximum limit was $7900 (individual option) and $15800 (family option). These figures may vary significantly, e.g. in the health insurance of company A the limit may be $2000, and in company B it may be $6000. However, neither of them can exceed the maximum values.

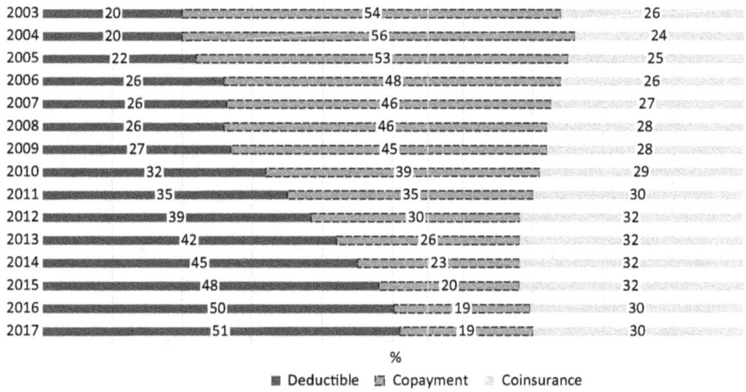

Figure 2.6 Percentage distribution of types of direct payments in 2003–2017.

Source: Own study based on: Rae, Copeland & Cox, 2019.

Note: The survey was carried out in large enterprises, i.e., employing more than 200 employees, and concerned insurance included in the family option.

The observed trends are, among others, the aftermath of the increase in insurance premiums in the 1990s. The insured are more sensitive to the costs of medical services resulting from deductibles or coinsurance than in the case of copayment which is a predetermined rate. In addition, the copayment can be spread over time depending on what services the insured will use. In the case of the deductible, there is no such possibility, as it is the amount that determines the limit of costs that the insured person incurs in the first place (Rae, Copeland & Cox, 2019). Therefore, for insurance companies, the deductible has become a very useful and thus more willingly used tool in limiting the consumption of benefits by the insured.

Rising premiums are also a growing problem for employers, especially those with 3-9 employees. In 2019, only 47% of companies offered health insurance. In smaller companies, i.e., those in which earnings are relatively lower than in larger entities, employees also have a higher level of deductible, averaging $2,271 compared to $1,412 in entities with more than 200 employees (the average for all companies is $1,655) (Kaiser Family Foundation, 2019a, p. 11). Employers also reduce insurance costs by increasing the share of employees in the premium paid. Due to the reliefs to which they are entitled, this does not meet with strong opposition, but it undoubtedly reduces their real wages. The share of the employee part in the total health insurance premium is increased for both individual and family options (Figure 2.7).

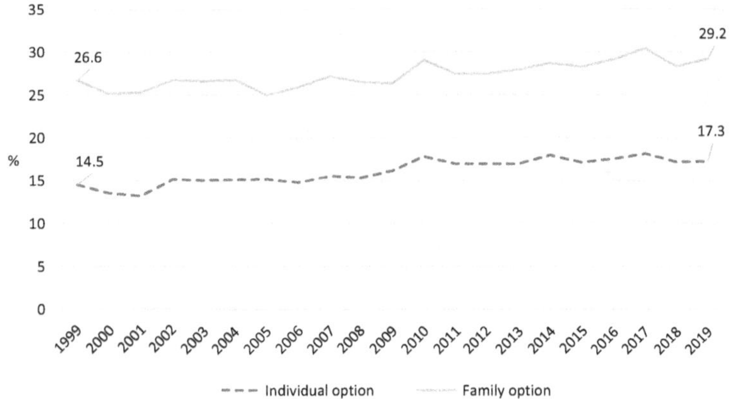

Figure 2.7 The proportion of the contribution paid by employees as a percentage of the total contribution.

Source: Own study based on: Kaiser Family Foundation, 2019c.

High deductible health plan with saving option

To support their employees in covering growing expenses not covered by insurance, some employers offer special types of health plans. These plans are called High Deductible Health Plan with Saving Option (HDHP/SO). While the deductible is higher, the employee pays a lower premium than with other types of plans (Figure 2.8). On the other hand, resources intended for higher direct expenditure are linked to a special account allowing tax preferences related to the revenues allocated to these expenditures.[7] With these accounts, the cost of the deductible, among other things, is covered. The two most common accounts are Health Reimbursement Arrangements (HRA) and Health Savings Accounts (HSA). According to KFF's assumptions, any plan with a minimum deductible of $1,000 (individual option) and $2,000 (family option) is an HDHP plan linked to an HRA account. On the other hand, the deductible limits that determine the classification of health plans as HDHP associated with HSA are determined by federal regulations (Kaiser Family Foundation, 2019a, p. 139). For instance, in 2020, the IRS set the minimum deductible for an HDHP/HSA plan at $1,400 (individual option) and $2,800[8] (family option) (HealthCare.gov, n.d.).

More and more employers are using this solution. The number of companies offering them increased from 4% in 2005 to 28% in 2019.[9] This also translated to an increase in the number of employees covered by such plans. While in 2006 such solutions were used by 4% of employees, in 2019 their share increased to 30%.[10] This is one of the reasons for the significant increase in the amount of deductible.

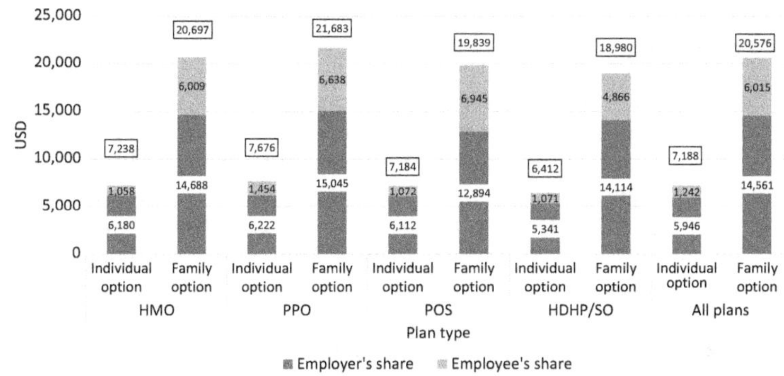

Figure 2.8 Premiums for each type of health insurance plan in 2019.

Source: Own study based on: Kaiser Family Foundation, 2019a, p. 8.

Note: Other types of health plans (with lower deductibles) include Health Maintenance Organization (HMO), Preferred Provider Organization (PPO), Point of Service (POS), and Conventional plans.

However, the authors of the report on occupational health insurance point out that, while in the case of Preferred Provider Organization (PPO) and other deductibles serve their purpose by increasing the liability of the insured, in the case of HDHP/SO plans this tool may not be as effective. This is because many employees enrolled in these plans receive from their employers' financial allowances which go into their HRA/HSA accounts. 21% of employees with an HDHP/HRA plan (individual option) and 2% of employees with an HDHP/HSA plan receive such an allowance amounting to at least the deductible. Another 22% of employees with an HDHP/HRA plan and 23% with an HDHP/HSA plan receive allowances that reduce their deductibles to $1,000 (Kaiser Family Foundation, 2019a, pp. 140–142). In fact, these actions indicate the room for manoeuvre available to employers is limited. Just as health insurance should not be seen as an instrument to cover all medical expenses, a higher deductible and other forms of direct payments should not be a reason for further support from employers, as this reduces the effectiveness of these plans, further leading to a vicious circle of rising health insurance costs.

The percentage of employees enrolled in each type of plan in companies offering one type of health plan in 2019 was: HDHP/SO (27%), POS (9%), PPO (52%), HMO (12%), Conventional (<1%).

These plans vary in rates/direct payment rates, grace periods, medical coverage plan, and choices of physicians and other services within or outside the network. PPO and POS plans offer the opportunity to use medical services outside of a given network.

Tax privileges as one of the reasons for the increase in health insurance costs

As it has already been mentioned, the ongoing trend of increasing direct expenditure on health insurance may cause some difficulties in the situation of a slower rate of wage growth, for example, for people with relatively low savings. Furthermore, rising direct expenditure can also be felt when overall health care costs are rising at a moderate rate (Saywer, Cox & Claxton, 2017). However, this results from basing the financing of access to medical services mainly on occupational health insurance and strong and long-term constraints on the supply side.

Americans do not have a bad opinion of their employee health plans. After all, they provide them with a range of benefits at a fraction of the cost. The deductible is not a foreign body in the world of health insurance, but its indispensable part that allows to maintain a more rational consumption by requiring the insured to cover fewer medical expenses. Despite this, the use of such tools is not understood and favourably received by the insured. One of the reasons for this is undoubtedly the higher costs they must incur. The second important reason is that the costs of the deductible are not treated as an insurance premium, so, as a result, although they are paid by employees, this cost does not constitute a contribution to the tax relief, as is the case with the part of the premium paid by employees. From the employees' perspective, these are somewhat unproductive expenses, because there are no tax benefits. That is why many people look favourably on expanding the scope of insurance to include routine procedures that increase the amount of premiums, as this also increases their tax relief (Galles, 2018). This also explains the growing popularity of HDHP/SO plans.

In this context, it is worth paying attention to who ends up paying the increasingly higher bill for health insurance. There are two groups of people who can be identified here: the employees themselves and the taxpayers. For employees, the situation seems clear. Insurance covers most of their expenses, part of the premium paid by the employer is exempt from taxes, and part of the premium paid by employees counts as a tax relief. However, the costs, in fact, come back to the employees in the form of increasing premiums or, for example, deductibles. Even if the employer increases their share in the contribution, it is at the expense of, for example, an increase in the employee's salary. Moreover, from an economic point of view, the division into the part of the contribution paid by the employer and the employee is not set, since eventually it cannot be higher than the employee's marginal productivity (the same applies to wages). The employer does not have an additional pool of funds allocated to insurance – everything can be reduced to the premium-salary relationship. An employee who uses health insurance believes that it is done at zero or minimal cost, when in fact his actions are driving up costs for other employees who are doing the same. Eventually, it is impossible to pass on the costs to others without the same actions on their part. This can be compared, for example, to a situation at a football match, when one of the fans gets up to observe the events on the pitch from a better position, but at the same time makes it difficult for several people who are seated to have a good view. If more and more people start doing the same, then in the end they all go back to the starting point, except that they were sitting before and are now they are standing, which further increases their discomfort.

Nevertheless, employees benefit from the tax benefits which they are entitled to. However, there may also be a mechanism of cost passing-on. For the federal budget, exemptions from income taxes and payroll taxes are the source of a significant shortfall in tax revenues – these are the so-called tax expenditures (TEs). TEs can be defined as losses in budget revenue resulting from federal tax laws that allow special exclusions, exemptions, deductions from gross income, or provide a special relief, preferential tax rate, or deferral of tax liability (Department Of the Treasury (n.d.). There are many types of TEs in the USA. One of the largest (in fiscal terms) include:

- exclusion of employer-paid health insurance premiums from federal income taxes,
- exclusion of gross rent income from taxable income from housing services,
- preferential tax rates on capital gains and dividends, and
- deferring taxes on contributions and profits made in employees' retirement accounts until they retire.[11]

As far as occupational health insurance is concerned, the value of exclusions for the part of the contribution paid by employers from income taxes and payroll taxes in 2018 amounted to $337 billion, $205 billion of which related to income tax exemptions.[12] By comparison, the federal deficit for 2018 was $779 billion, equivalent to 3.9% of GDP. The total value of these exemptions thus accounted for 43% of the total deficit and corresponded to approximately 1.7% of GDP. This is because the two taxes mentioned above are the largest sources of federal revenue, having generated a combined 88%[13] of total budget revenues in 2018 (Congressional Budget Office, 2019a). Interestingly, according to the latest calculations by the Treasury Department, the value of these two exemptions is expected to increase significantly this decade. According to estimates, the value of exclusions from income taxes alone in 2029 is expected to amount to over $438 billion, and payroll taxes to an additional $235 billion (Department of The Treasury, 2020).

This is problematic for two reasons. First, the higher the aggregates resulting from these tax exemptions, the more money goes back into a poorly designed (overly regulated) system based on occupational health insurance, leading to further overconsumption and a renewed increase in insurance costs. In such institutional circumstances, the above-mentioned tax preferences, as well as the tax relief obtained by employees, do not play a due role. This is not to provide an argument for abolishing these benefits but to draw attention to the cost-increasing flow path. It would seem rational to abolish many of the state regulations in effect.

Second, the federal government is more willing to impose new taxes or increase the deficit (and national debt) to compensate for lost revenue. At the end of the day, the additional costs of occupational health insurance are borne by the economy and taxpayers. Some of them are the same employees who previously received tax privileges. However, this is not so noticeable for them because the new burdens are spread over time and involve more people. Only if the government reduced total spending by an amount equal to lost revenue would the costs not be passed on to taxpayers. It is unlikely that the federal government will abandon some of its planned spending for other purposes. In U.S. history, federal deficits are more common than non-existent. This is not to change in the years to come either. The Congressional Budget Office estimated the deficit in 2019 at $896 billion. By 2029, it is expected to increase to $1.3 trillion, which will increase the share of the deficit in the U.S. GDP from 4.2% to 4.5% (Congressional Budget Office, 2019b).

Employee retirement income security act

State regulations artificially expanded health insurance coverage and curtailed insurance companies' methods of reducing moral hazard. For many employers, especially for smaller companies, health insurance became a source of increasing costs. Therefore, the so-called self-insurance option became a viable and increasingly popular alternative to health insurance. However, this solution required further changes in the law. These came in 1974 with the Employee Retirement Income Security Act (ERISA) and its subsequent amendments. According to the Act, employers themselves act as insurers by creating their own health plans. Thus, it is the employer's responsibility to finance employees' access to medical benefits, although the process of managing expenses for these purposes may be outsourced to an external entity, for example, an insurance company. This service is called Administered Service Only (ASO). Full financial responsibility lies with the employer (and not with the insurer) who is obliged to provide adequate funds for these purposes. These funds are transferred to a special fund. Nevertheless, this solution is more popular in large enterprises due to their better financial capabilities.

The Acts provides employers with several benefits unattainable with typical health insurance. They include the abolition of state coverage requirements (e.g., the requirement to insure against rare diseases or certain services provided by specific interest groups) or the exemption of such plans from state taxes on insurance premiums paid by insurance companies. For a complete list of the benefits of self-insurance plans, see Table 2.2. Some of these benefits were like those granted to the Blue Cross and Blue Shield plans in the 1930s. This meant that self-insurance had to meet additional requirements: a prohibition of discriminating against higher and lower-wage employees in the provision of benefits (Congressional Budget Office, 1994, pp. 5–6). It should also be remembered that when creating such a plan, the company must consider the alternative of insurance. If, for example, they reduce their benefits, employees may be dissatisfied and may even leave for a competitor.

However, time has shown that these benefits significantly outweigh the limitations, which has led to a growing popularity of this type of solution on the part of enterprises, especially those employing thousands of employees. According to KFF data, in 2019 as many as 61% of all employees used self-insurance plans. It is also characteristic that this percentage is significantly higher in companies with more than 1000 employees (86%) compared to companies with less than 200 employees (17%) (Kaiser Family Foundation, 2019a, p. 171). This should not come as a

Table 2.2 Benefits for employers of self-insured plans

Benefits	*Description*
Greater flexibility	An employer can tailor a plan to meet employees' specific health needs, as opposed to purchasing universal insurance.
Interest benefit	The employer may benefit from its own maintenance of financial reserves, e.g., in the form of interest on deposits. Otherwise, the income would be invested by the insurer without sharing the profit with the employer.
Better liquidity	The employer does not have to pay in advance for given services, which ensures a better flow of funds in the company.
Abolition of state regulations	Self-financed plans are governed by federal law (ERISA), so they do not have to comply with state requirements such as insurance coverage.
Tax benefits	State insurance premium taxes of about 2–3% are not levied on employers' premiums.
Better collaboration with suppliers	An employer may enter into an agreement with suppliers or a network of suppliers that is best suited to the health needs of their employees.

Source: Own study based on: Self-Insurance Institute of America, n.d.

surprise, given that most of the insured employees are employed by larger companies. Other sources say that out of a total of 176 million people receiving access to medical services, 60% of employees and their families (about 105 million) were covered by their employers with such plans (in 2016). As it turns out, such solutions are effective because they allow employers to reduce costs and at the same time take care of the health of their employees (Goldberg, Fragala & Wohlgemuth, 2019, pp. 547–548; Barnett & Berchick, 2017, p. 4). By comparison, according to the Employee Benefit Research Institute (EBRI), in 2000 about 50 million employees and their families were covered by such plans (Self-Insurance Institute of America, n.d.).

To lower the risk of high costs and financial losses, many of these plans include an additional option, the so-called stoploss, which sets a maximum limit on the employer's liability. If it is exceeded, the costs are taken over by the insurer. In a way, this allows insurers to recoup some of the lost revenue due to the lack of health insurance sales.

The growing popularity of self-insurance options has also translated into the development of this type of offer for small businesses.[14] This is how the level funded, i.e., self-insurance plans were created, which, unlike the plans of larger companies, offers lower levels of insurer's liability (the so-called *attachment points*). The fees for this type of financial service resemble insurance premiums, however, the basic principle of this plan is the same as that of the stoploss option. This allows companies with smaller revenues to reduce costs. According to estimates, in 2019 about 7% of companies with fewer than 200 employees had level funded plans (Kaiser Family Foundation, 2019a, p. 170, 174).

Other ways to reduce health care costs

The highest costs of medical services are generated by hospitals and doctors, which is why alternative entities that could offer some of these services in the appropriate quality, but at a relatively lower cost are being sought. In 82% of companies with 50 or more employees, medical services are also provided by retail clinics located in pharmacies, supermarkets or retail stores. Such facilities are mainly staffed by physician assistants and nurses who deal with minor illnesses and provide preventive services. Many companies also have in their health plans telemedicine services or facilities in convenient locations (Kaiser Family Foundation, 2019a, pp. 15–16).

The growth of retail clinics and their competition has made physicians in many states, especially the American Medical Association (AMA), put pressure on them. The AMA's activities are focused on limiting the range of services provided by such networks. This is done at the state level by regulating the range of services that, for example, nurses can provide. AS a result, some medical services cannot be provided in these facilities without the participation of doctors. However, such actions do not always bring the intended results. For instance, more than 20 states have passed laws allowing nurses to do their jobs without a doctor's supervision, including prescribing medication (this is called a *full practice authority*). Eventually, doctors failed to prevent competition for several reasons. First, many entities count on the development of the market, from large retail chains (CVS Health and Walgreens) through smaller chains, other doctors, to established institutions such as the Mayo Clinic. The number of entities willing to cooperate is constantly increasing, which makes monopolistic activities on the part of the AMA more difficult. Secondly, large chains can afford to (counter)lobby thanks to their financial capabilities. Third, the AMA gives the impression that the main reason for its decisive action is to maintain the relatively high salaries of doctors. Fourthly, surveys on the quality and satisfaction with the services provided confirm the high standards of services provided by retail clinics (Hyman & Silver, 2018, pp. 329–330).

It is particularly important that a health plan in the form of self-insurance allows one to bypass the intermediary in the form of an insurer and use the services of providers directly. Competition from retail clinics has also led to positive effects in the form of price reductions by some doctors associated in private medical practices. As it turns out, the difference in prices is huge and with cheaper competition, it is difficult for previously privileged entities to maintain their position (Hyman & Silver, 2018, p. 331).

Another example is the dynamic development of specialist medical centres which offer many treatments to their patients directly, outside the insurance system, at relatively low prices. The Surgery Center of Oklahoma (SCO) specializes in such activities. For instance, sinus surgery at SCO costs $5,885, compared to the $33,505 one must pay at Integris[15] who has been in the market for a longer time. And this is the price only for the hospitalization itself.[16] Such a big price difference results mainly from the costs generated by hospitals. This price includes $360 for a steroid available in bulk for just 75 cents, and $630 for three doses of painkiller, for which the hospital pays about $1.50. Further examples can be multiplied. One hospital in California estimated the cost of a CT scan at $6,707, of which the insured employee paid $2,336 out of pocket.[17] If the payment had been made at a retail clinic, the total cost would have been $1054. Similarly, a hospital in Colorado charged the insured $600 for an X-ray, but only $70 for direct payment outside of insurance. If the same person needed an MRI sometime later, own costs from insurance would be $1,100, but $600 for cash payment. Yet another Michigan entity charges patients $510 for an HDHP plan, but only $265 for direct payment outside of insurance (Hyman & Silver, 2018, pp. 323–333).

These examples are no exceptions and occur throughout the country. The financing of even low-cost services by hospitals with monopolistic privileges leads to skyrocketing costs. The gravity of this situation is illustrated by numerous examples where services purchased directly are much cheaper than those offered by health insurance, which clearly contradicts the whole idea of buying insurance. Therefore, the development of the retail clinic market should be considered a very important trend that may change the structure of financing access to medical services in the USA. The above examples also clearly demonstrate that the lack of health insurance does not mean huge costs, and that the processes of competition have a positive impact on all market participants. Health insurance does not guarantee the affordability that many Americans dream of. Nor is it unusual to say that such a regulated insurance institution ultimately misleads uninformed policyholders (consumers) about the costs. Indeed, when the price falls, the quantity purchased for the goods and services in question increases. In this case, the results of the now famous health experiment conducted in the 1970s by the RAND institution should not be surprising. In the face of the achievements of economic theory, they are not. A study of 7,700 people found that when their costs rise, the number of medical services they use decreases.[18] This research is not a confirmation of the theory, it is the theory that confirms the said experiment, enabling proper understanding of its value.

Insurance companies themselves are also aware of the existing problems and are taking measures to better assess and manage risks. They search for more unconventional methods, for example, in the form of alternative medicine. A breakthrough (in the mid-1990s) for this type of practice was the decision that the Mutual of Omaha Insurance Company, the largest insurer in the individual health insurance market, would reimburse policyholders if they decided to participate in a then-innovative programme that combined a healthy diet, meditation and exercise to treat heart disease. It was a so-called *reversal programme* developed by Dr Dean Ornish, director of the Research Institute for Preventive Medicine in Sausalito, to completely cure the disease, not just slow its progression. This sparked interest in this and similar plans offered by other insurance companies. Costs turned out to be crucial. Dr Ornish's plan involved an expense of $3,500 per year, which constituted 10% of the cost of traditional coronary artery disease treatment. It is important because coronary artery bypass surgery is very expensive in the USA and, thus, it constitutes one of the highest costs for insurers (O'Neill, n.d.). For these entities, this meant a reduction in costs, and it significantly influenced the development of solutions focused on activating the insured to take care of their own health, thus reducing insurance risk. Nowadays, there are many more similar solutions.

Many employers also have programmes to help employees identify health problems and treat chronic diseases, including health risk assessments, biometric testing, and health promotion programmes. For instance, in 2019 41% of small businesses and 65% of large companies provided employees with the opportunity to complete a health risk assessment programme. This assessment includes questions about the individual's medical history, health status, and lifestyle. To that end, 51% of large companies have introduced incentives for employees, such as gift cards, merchandise or similar rewards, lower premiums or financial rewards in the form of cash. Additionally, 14% of large companies with biometric screening programmes reward or penalize their employees based on specific biometric results, such as reaching a target BMI. The size of these incentives varies. Among the 17% of large companies offering rewards and penalties for getting the right biometric results, the maximum reward is $150, while a reward of $1000 or higher is offered by 11% of them (Kaiser Family Foundation, 2019a, p. 14).

Medical tourism as a real alternative to expensive treatment in the USA

The self-financing option gave some employers more opportunities to choose the right solutions to support their employees in the treatment process and reduce costs. In this case, one can talk about groundbreaking initiatives used by more and more entities (companies). Employers turned their attention to the dynamically developing medical tourism market. The benefits they derived from working with retail clinics were one of the reasons for looking for less expensive options for more serious medical services as well, such as more complex surgeries that required more time and a longer rehabilitation process. In the USA, these services are mainly provided by hospitals, but their cost is a huge problem. Hence, employers (and insurance companies) started looking for alternatives outside the USA as well. In this case, the advantage of foreign clinics over the American ones is that the model of a network of retail clinics has also been applied to surgeries or other major procedures, and not only to less advanced services.

The development of the global medical tourism market is extremely dynamic, and Americans also have their own share. As recently as 2007, about 750,000 of them were travelling abroad for medical purposes. According to Patient Beyond Borders, an institution that researches this market, in 2017 there were already 1.4 million of them. According to estimates, in 2020 it will be about 2.2 million people from the USA. The main reason is the high cost of medical services in the USA. The growth rate for the global medical tourism market is estimated at 15–25% per year. In monetary terms, the value of this market is estimated in the range of $74–92 billion, and the total number of patients is to be 21–26 million people who spend an average of $3,555 per visit (Patient Beyond Borders, n.d.). For businesses in many countries, the influx of tourists travelling for medical purposes means more revenue than for a regular tourism business. Israel is a good example. According to a report by Israel's Ministry of Health, in 2013 a medical tourist spent an average of $5,000 per capita in the country compared to $1,500 spent by ordinary tourists (Patient Beyond Borders, n.d.). Particularly impressive is the wide range of services offered and their relatively low prices which are lower by several dozen percent compared to the prices in the USA (Table 2.3).

The range of services provided is very wide, which is a response to the diverse needs of patients and competition between individual countries. The key factor, of course, is the cost. The average savings on the cost of medical services in individual countries compared to prices in the USA are substantial. Furthermore, Americans benefit not only from the significantly lower costs of these services but also from a relatively convenient location (e.g., Costa Rica or Mexico).

Interestingly, developed countries also offer much lower prices. Dr Martin Makary (Johns Hopkins University) gives the example of an American who was diagnosed with a mild heart attack in the emergency department. Then, after his condition was stabilized, he was offered bypass surgery. However, its potential cost was as high as $150,000, which

Table 2.3 Scope and costs of medical services offered in individual countries compared to the USA

Most popular destinations (in the alphabetical order)	*Average savings range compared to prices in the USA*
Brazil	20–30%
Costa Rica	45–65%
India	65–90%
Israel	n.d.
Malaysia	65–80%
Mexico	40–65%
Singapore	25–40%
South Korea	35–40%
Taiwan	40–45%
Thailand	50–75%
Turkey	50–65%

Most popular medical services:
Cosmetic surgery, dentistry, procedures performed on the cardiovascular system, orthopaedic services, cancer treatment, infertility treatment, weight loss procedures, and diagnostic services.

Source: own study based on: Patient Beyond Borders, n.d.

was beyond the financial capabilities of the patient's family. Therefore, they started looking for cheaper options abroad. The efforts paid off, as they got in touch with a surgeon in France who was willing to perform the procedure in the same quality for \$15,000. When the hospital representative learned of plans for an operation in France which would be ten times cheaper, he began to lower the price of the procedure at the hospital in the USA, first going down to \$50,000 and later to \$25,000. However, the family and the patient were so outraged by the situation that they decided to have the operation in France anyway (Makary, 2019, pp. 41–43). This example illustrates very well the positive impact of foreign competition on the prices offered by domestic institutions with monopolistic privileges.

Equally important is the development of accreditation institutions that care about the quality of services offered and thus the safety of patients. In the USA, one of such institutions is the Joint Commission (JC) which accredits thousands of medical entities and services. In response to the growing demand for medical tourism services, JC has established the Joint Commission International (JCI) for the accreditation of international hospitals. To be accredited by the JCI, a foreign hospital must meet the same set of stringent requirements as hospitals in the USA. Currently, more than 950 hospitals and clinical units around the world have managed to receive such accreditation, and their number is growing by about 20% per year. This means that the services offered are not only less expensive, but also, just as importantly, they are of adequate quality. The situation is similar in the case of outpatient clinics. Agencies such as The Accreditation Association of Ambulatory Health Care (AAAHC) and the American Association for Accreditation of Ambulatory Surgery Facilities (AAASF), which accredit clinics across the USA, have also launched their international outpatient care initiatives (Patient Beyond Borders, n.d.). In addition, people who decide to undergo treatment abroad can buy insurance against complications, which reduces the risk of incurring costs in the future.

In addition to accreditation institutions, the USA. is witnessing the development of many intermediary entities offering Americans a range of services related to medical tourism, such as organization of the admission process to foreign hospitals and doctors, air travel, hotel accommodation, and providing basic information about treatment abroad. In 2008, there were more than 60 institutions in the USA dealing with such services. Interestingly, major American medical centres such as Harvard University, Boston University, Johns Hopkins University, and Cleveland Clinic have also established their own hospitals and clinics outside the USA to take over part of the share in the dynamically developing market (Dalen & Alpert, 2019, pp. 9–10). Such a development may be quite surprising for some, as the USA may well be indicated as the destination of medical tourism for other nations.

In the context of the discussed issues, employers have also begun to play the role of intermediaries. The relatively low costs have attracted the attention of companies with health plans based on self-insurance. The company that first paved the way for this type of practice was the furniture manufacturer HSM Solutions based in the state of New York. Due to the profile of the company's business, the company's employees had problems with spinal injuries. The standard treatment of, for example, intervertebral disc injuries was repeated from time to time and thus tiring. Meanwhile, doctors in India performed total intervertebral disc replacement while maintaining the patient's mobility. According to the company's estimates, in the USA, the cost of such an operation would be \$300,000–\$400,000 compared to \$38,000 (including the \$5,000 ticket price) in India. Within a few years of the first trip of this type, several hundred employees of the company and their family members benefited from similar services. To create appropriate incentives for their employees, the company took several other important measures, including not charging them with their own expenses, financing the travel costs of employees and accompanying persons, and paying a bonus of 20% of the amount saved. Compared to the cost of a few hundred or a few thousand dollars for treatment in the USA, it was a positive change for the employees. All these benefits were possible thanks to the large savings that the company could achieve thanks to cheaper treatment abroad – according to estimates, it was about \$9.5 million in the first 6 years from the introduction of this solution. Later, the list of offered treatments was constantly expanding, including such procedures as: bariatric surgeries, knee and hip replacement, hernia surgeries or endoscopy of knees and shoulders, which are performed in Costa Rica,[19] closer to the USA, where, as it turned out, these services were even cheaper than in India (Wojcik, 2013).

These positive experiences led to more and more employers adopting these solutions. Thus, a certain circular process of moving away from the use of health insurance can be observed, from which employers and their employees clearly benefit. In a way, this is also due to self-insurance which does not prohibit this type of practice.

The growth of the medical tourism market is leading to a scale of cost reduction that is difficult to imagine in the USA. A good example is LASIK – laser vision correction. In the USA, this service is relatively cheap anyway, as it is not subject to third-party financing in the same way as cosmetic surgery services. However, the price comparison of this service in 2015 is in favour of India, where its cost was \$1,000 compared to \$4,000 in the USA. This demonstrates the potential of this market. Another noteworthy case is the Narayana Hrudayalaya Hospital in India which specializes in heart surgery. By providing services on a massive scale, the cost of coronary artery bypass grafting was reduced to about \$2,000, which is a huge achievement not only compared to the USA

($123,000 in 2015), but also in the domestic market, where the average price for such a procedure was around $5,000 at the time. This institution is headed by Dr Devi Shetty, an Indian cardiac surgeon, entrepreneur, and philanthropist. The hospital uses price differentiation as its business strategy. For foreign and wealthier clients, the cost of such a service is several thousand dollars, which at the same time allows the indigenous population to be offered insurance for this type of treatment, costing them several dozen or even several cents per month. Mortality rates of 1.4% compared to 1.9% in the USA are also impressive. There is a reason why Dr Shetty has been dubbed *the Henry Ford of Heart Surgery* by *The Wall Street Journal.* In fact, the number of procedures performed in his centre reaches a massive scale. The number of hospitals has grown to more than a dozen units across India, with a monthly number of procedures performed at around 24,000 (Quirk, 2017, pp. 491, 501–502, 511–512).

This is not the only case of this kind. Another example is Aravind Eye Hospitals (AEH), one of the largest eye hospitals in the world, founded by Dr Govindapp Venkataswamy. Venkataswamy started by setting up mobile clinics to reach small and remote villages with its services. This project was carried out in collaboration with the Royal Commonwealth Society for the Blind and the Government of India. However, his greatest contribution to the improvement of the health of the population was possible thanks to the establishment of the Aravind Eye Hospital – a small hospital at the beginning, which quickly developed into a very large activity. According to a study conducted by Harvard Business School, having been established in 1976, by 1992 it had examined about 3.65 million people and performed 335,000 cataract surgeries. Almost 70% of these surgeries were carried out at a very low cost or completely free of charge to the poor. The business model is like D. Shetty's business – it is based on reducing costs by achieving the largest possible scale of operations (Sanandaji, 2020, p. 31).[20]

There are many more such examples, and they prove that in improving the availability of medical services competitive and dynamic market processes leading to a systematic reduction of costs while increasing the scale of operations are much more effective than universal insurance.

Difficult cooperation between insurance companies and hospitals

It is often thought that the insurance market is the main driver behind rising health care costs. Such judgments do not consider the role of state and federal regulations or supply constraints. American hospitals are largely responsible for the latter.

One of the hallmarks of the American hospital system is the lack of prices. Receiving certain hospital services financed by the insurer, a patient cannot estimate their cost and does not even feel the need to do so. They cannot, therefore, properly assess how much they would have to pay for them out of their own pocket. This is, among other things, the result of negotiations between hospitals and insurers. In most cases, state regulations do not require suppliers (hospitals) to disclose prices. As Nicholas DeSimone of the Reason Foundation points out, such practices lead to huge disparities in the pricing of the most common medical procedures (i.e., appendectomy, hysterectomy, caesarean section, or knee replacement) by different hospitals. In California, for example, an appendectomy costs anywhere from $1,529 to $182,955, depending on where the procedure is performed. However, the reason is not the differences in the cost of these treatments, but the monopolistic privileges of some hospitals (DeSimone, 2018).

Importantly, insurance companies cannot take advantage of cheaper competitors (as is the case with retail clinic chains) for two reasons. Firstly, there may simply be a shortage of them in a given area. Secondly, hospitals with the most facilities within their networks and a monopoly position can use them to limit competition from other suppliers through restrictive requirements in contracts with insurers. An example of this is the agreement between Cigna Corp and New York-Presbyterian Hospital, which stipulated that the insurer could not use the additional services of a competing provider, Northwell Health, to reduce costs. The insurer could also not sign a contract only with a cheaper supplier, because the latter simply did not have the appropriate number of facilities (Wilde Mathews, 2018).

Paradoxically, the increase in the prices of hospital services also results from the fact that individual entities merge their activities. Higher prices are found in large hospital chains which are the only service providers in a given area, as well as in specialized hospitals. Such entities, due to the scale of their operations and the level of specialization, must be included in the health plans of insurers as key providers. Ultimately, this translates into higher health insurance prices. In an unregulated market, consolidation brings benefits in the form of positive economies of scale and cost reductions. This is the economic sense of business mergers, but in a regulated market the effects are entirely different. It also has a negative impact on the largest companies in the USA, where due to restrictive provisions in contracts between hospitals and insurers, even large entities such as Walmart and Home Depot have not been able to implement their own plans to reduce health care costs (Consumers for Quality Care, 2018). This is one of the reasons why medical tourism is gaining so much importance.

This situation also contributes to the misperception of the true nature of the American health care system by European health care politicians and policymakers. This is well reflected in the statement of Tom Sackville

(2013, p. 98), former Minister of Health of the United Kingdom made during his stay in Poland:

> Let me now present the other side of this system, namely the potential dangers of a real market system for healthcare. I wanted to show you this slide because that is the result of putting in place a system that does not try to regulate healthcare providers in any way to control costs. It is a survey carried out annually by the federation. The number on the right – $1,121 – is the average price paid in the U.S. industrial market, i.e., by the 150 million Americans with private health insurance, for an MRI. So, in Baltimore, you pay $1121 for a procedure that costs $319 in Rotterdam. The American people have a free market, which is great, but they haven't been able to find a way to stop doctors and hospitals from introducing cartels and monopolies. As in our country, politicians in the United States are afraid of doctors because they are the ones who win the political races. That's why the Federal Trade Commission isn't targeting healthcare providers because people are paying more than they should for an MRI. Despite the outrageousness of such a system, no one in the White House plans to do anything about it. We can assume that many well-known American politicians receive sizable political campaign donations from hospital associations, medical associations, and the pharmaceutical industry. This is an interesting kind of system. So, if you plan to follow this market path, you will have to rely on more than just market forces and prepare price regulations for all healthcare services.

Although this statement contains some true and important observations in some respects, the conclusions it ultimately leads to are fundamentally wrong, and the very assessment of the American system is very unfair. In fact, this statement is the result of a very superficial analysis that does not adequately reflect the true situation.

Firstly, the USA is perceived by many European politicians as a country where the state does not significantly interfere in the economy. America is primarily associated with freedom and capitalism.

Secondly, Sackville makes no reference at all to the existence of many government institutions (at the federal and state levels) and regulations that significantly affect virtually every part of the U.S. health care system: the AMA, the FDA, Medicare, Medicaid, non-market hospitalization, insurer regulation, and so on. In fact, there are very few areas where such interventions are few, such as the retail clinic market or the cosmetic surgery market.

Thirdly, there is no reference to the dynamic nature of interventionism, the development of the powers of those institutions that do not operate to a limited extent away from the market, but are constantly expanding the scope of their powers, such as the FDA.

Fourthly, and this is particularly important, this and other statements often confuse the legal form of institutions (e.g., insurance companies) with the scope of regulations to which they are subject. The fact that from the point of view of the law they are private institutions does not mean that they operate in market conditions. From an economic point of view, the market works if the state does not intervene. In both the last and the present century, there was and has not been free market for medical services in the USA. Talking about high prices for individual services offered by private entities without referring to the sphere of regulation is prevaricating. High prices are the result of non-market regulations, but looking at market participants as formally private entities, one can get a different impression. Therefore, believing that in the U.S. market processes lead to significant price increases, Sackville suggests price controls as a means of counteracting such practices, forgetting or perhaps not even knowing that throughout the history of the U.S. health care system prices have been repeatedly controlled, which only made the situation worse. Nevertheless, it is true that the various interest groups he mentions enjoy their monopolistic privileges, which has its consequences in terms of high prices and restriction of competition. However, such actions are not part of unfettered market processes.

In fact, Sackville should blame the current situation on measures that effectively restrict the market. The whole statement could only be considered accurate if the participation of individual federal and state governments in this area was marginal from both the fiscal and regulatory perspectives, but this was not the case in the past and is not the case today.

Identity crisis of health insurance companies

The interventions described above are increasingly making it impossible for insurance companies to function properly. State regulations significantly limit their ability to properly assess the risks at the core of their business. On top of that, providers (hospitals) inflate prices or create their own health plans. Many employers also opt for self-insurance solutions, leaving administrative tasks to insurers. Retail clinic chains and medical tourism, where health insurance is not the main form of financing, are also developing.

The current conditions have thus led to a kind of identity crisis for insurers – as Bob Herman of Modern Healthcare described their current situation. In the face of these trends, insurers are facing a major challenge and are, in fact, forced to look for alternative opportunities to make profits. There are two main directions of these activities. The first is the area related to technology services. Some of the most significant insurers in the market,

UnitedHealth and Aetna, are the first to set new trends in the industry. For instance, UnitedHealth established Optum, a subsidiary that provides analytical, pharmaceutical, and consulting services to several organizations, while being the fastest-growing part of the group. Similar initiatives are also being developed by Aetna and other insurers (Herman, 2016).

The second, and perhaps even more important, direction is increasing engagement with the government's Medicare and Medicaid health programmes. However, this should not be so unusual, because private institutions with appropriate systems and quality management are better at providing services under such schemes than public entities. This is well illustrated by the change in the structure of insurers' revenues. For example, in 2007, commercial insurance premiums accounted for 87% of Aetna's total premiums, while Medicare and Medicaid premiums accounted for only 13% of the total. In 2017, the proportions were already 47–53% in favour of government programmes (Aetna, n.d., p. 5; Aetna, 2018, p. 56). The ongoing changes are also well illustrated by the data on the sources of revenue (2009–2019) of the largest American health insurer – UnitedHealth Group (Figure 2.9).

In the chart presented above one can observe a significant decline in the share of revenues from private insurance and an increase in the share of technology services (Optum). The total share of revenues from servicing government programmes increased slightly – from 46% in 2009 to 52% in 2019. That means only one in four dollars comes from private health

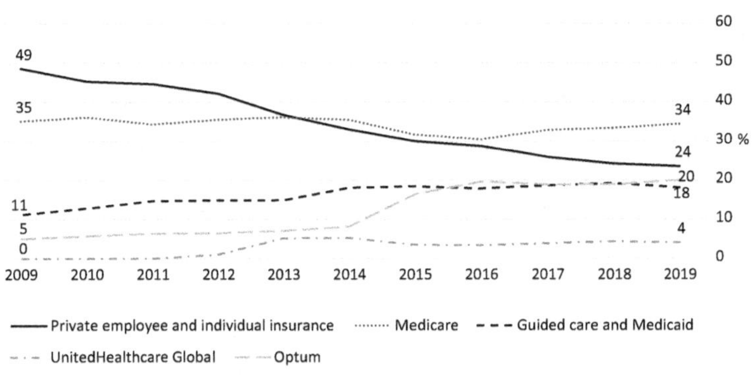

Figure 2.9 Changes in revenue sources (percentage) of the UnitedHealth Group.

Source: Own study based on: UnitedHealth Group, n.d.

Note: Optum is a subsidiary primarily providing technology services. It consists of three units: OptumHealth, which provides health and wellness services to residential, business, and government customers; OptumInsight, a provider of information, consulting and outsourcing software and services for the healthcare industry; OptumRx, which handles the processing and payment of prescription drugs. UnitedHealth Global is an entity that provides health services to governments, businesses, and individuals in more than 130 countries.[21]

insurance. In a sense, these results may be distorted by Optum's share. In this case, it is worth noting that there are significant differences in the growth of revenues from private and government insurance. Between 2009 and 2019, private insurance revenues grew by about 35%, Medicare revenues by 172%, and managed care[22] and Medicaid revenues by as much as 347% (UnitedHealth Group, n.d.).

According to a report prepared by PricewaterhouseCoopers (PwC), in 2016 private entities provided Medicaid health services to nearly 55 million people, which accounted for 73% of all beneficiaries. In 2013, the number of beneficiaries was 34 million, which marks an increase of 60%. For comparison, their number in other plans increased by less than 4% (in total it was 75.2 million people in 2016). It is also a result of the expansion of eligibility for this programme introduced by the ObamaCare reform. Insurance companies managing their costs better were good partners for individual states to implement this policy (Gottlieb, 2016, p. 3).

Another increasingly attractive business for insurers is Medicare Advantage plans, which provide the opportunity to receive Medicare benefits through private health plans, such as HMOs and PPOs, as an alternative to Medicare which is traditionally administered by the federal programme. The value of Medicare Advantage spending in 2019 was estimated at $250 billion, which accounted for about 33% of total spending. For insurers, in this case, the most important thing is to change the policy from one generating savings to one extending their benefits to beneficiaries after joining this type of plan (Kaiser Family Foundation, 2019b).

This encourages an increasing number of insurers to provide this type of service, which also translates into a growing number of beneficiaries. In 2019, 22 million (34%) of the 64 million total beneficiaries were enrolled in Medicare Advantage. This compares with 10.5 million (23%) in 2009 and 6.9 million (18%) in 1999. The prospects are also very promising. According to estimates by the Congressional Budget Office (CBO), the share of beneficiaries enrolled in Medicare Advantage is expected to increase to 49% in 2029, mainly due to the retirement of the generation of baby boomers (born between 1946 and 1964). In a sense, it can even be said that the government here is losing in its own backyard. That is why insurance companies did not hesitate and tried to increase their share in this market earlier. The largest shares of the Medicare Advantage market (2019) are held by the most significant health insurers: UnitedHealthcare (26%), Humana (18%), BlueCross/BlueShield (15%), and Aetna (10%). As a result, insurers can count on billions in profits. Interestingly, about 20% of people enrolled in Medicare Advantage (4.4 million) get this access through their employers or trade unions. These entities enter into agreements with insurers beforehand, whereby when an employee retires, Medicare pays the insurer a fixed amount for each enrolee to provide them with benefits guaranteed by Medicare (Jacobson et al., 2019).

Profits of health insurance companies

There is a lot of controversy over the profits of insurance companies, especially considering their financial difficulties. This is due to a misunderstanding of the profit function and misinterpretations of financial performance. Politicians often lament the high profits (and administrative costs) of insurance companies and propose that these surpluses should be used to increase spending on health care. Such opinions, however, ignore the benefits that the insured receive thanks to the activities of insurers.

An interesting analysis from this point of view was conducted by Chris Pope from the Manhattan Institute. Pope points to the problems with the costs generated by doctors or hospitals, while the activities of insurers require control of costs and claims. However, this allows for savings and better management of client funds. For instance, the efficient management of Medicare Advantage plans by private insurers makes them 10% less costly, which means about $1,000 in additional savings per beneficiary over the course of a year. Thanks to this, each of them can, for example, increase the range of services offered, the quality of care, etc. Nonetheless, this is the result of reasonable administration of costs and claims. In addition, such cost control reduces the cost of purchasing medical services (lower demand), thus, the benefits outweigh the costs. Furthermore, Pope cites data from the Centers for Medicare & Medicaid Services (CMS) and points out that in 2017, 34% of U.S. health care spending was spent on hospitals, 28% on medical services, 13% on nursing care, and 11% on prescription drugs. It is believed that it is not insurance per se that is the main factor in generating costs (Pope, 2019).

Thus, an attempt is made to counter the actions of insurers aimed at reducing costs and the actions of suppliers aimed at increasing them. However, one should remember that such an attempt to separate insurers from suppliers is not right. Insurance also has built-in elements that increase costs. That is why it is so important to assess risks, reduce moral hazard, etc. Nevertheless, as mentioned earlier, the use of these tools through government intervention has been reduced, so the insurance itself has become a significant source of increasing costs but on the demand side (rather than the supply side). This is not a criticism of the activity of insurers, but an attempt to draw attention to the fact that they operate in very limited conditions that do not result only from the actions of suppliers.

Criticism of the profits made by insurers is also unjustified and unfair. This can be illustrated with the words of Elizabeth Warren – a senator associated with the Democratic Party – during the preliminary presidential debate in the camp of the Democratic Party in 2019:

> The insurance companies last year alone sucked $23 billion in profits out of the health care system.[23]

This is misleading about the role that insurance companies play. First, although the figure of total profits is true, it says nothing about the profitability of the business. To an average person this amount may seem enormous, but not necessarily to insurers operating with billions of dollars. One of the main indicators that well illustrates the financial situation of health insurers (and not only) is the return on sales. As it turns out, net profits of $23 billion accounted for only 3.3% of insurers' premium revenues in 2018, and in the years 2009–2018 this ratio was in the range of 0.6–3.4%. The profits of 2018 are also record-breaking, as they amounted to $16 billion a year earlier and $7 billion in 2016 (Figure 2.10). With such profitability, a few percent drops in revenues or increases in costs can lead to losses. Thus, by giving the figure from 2018, Warren reinforces her political message rather than reflects the true picture of reality.

Secondly, while complaining about insurers' excessive profits, Warren does not consider that some of them come from servicing government programmes such as Medicare and Medicaid which mainly benefit their beneficiaries. It is true that it contributes to greater profits for insurers, but the profit is the effect of exchange. It is a win-win situation for both sides. This is especially evident in the case of Medicare Advantage, where seniors have a choice, and the programmes offered by insurers give them more benefits and are more innovative (Japsen, 2019).

Thirdly, insurers do not make billions in profits through a relatively large number of refusals to pay claims, which translates into growing profits. This is demonstrated by indicators such as *loss ratio* or *combined ratio*.

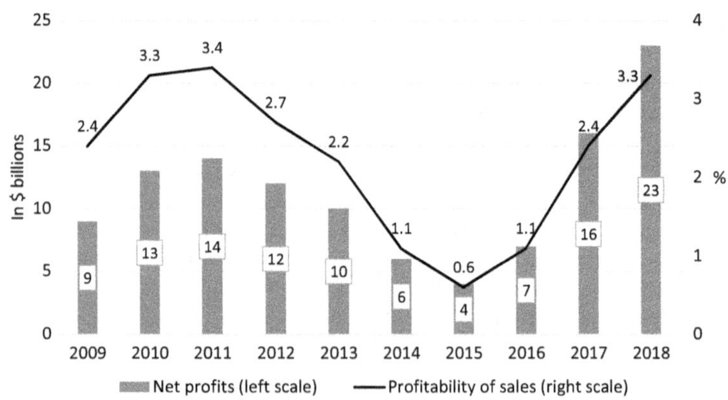

Figure 2.10 Total net profits and profitability of sales of health insurers.

Source: Own study based on: National Association of Insurance Commissioners, 2019, p. 2.

The *loss ratio* is the ratio of the sum of claims paid and the costs of corrections to the sum of premiums obtained (expressed as a percentage). On the other hand, the *combined ratio* is the ratio of the sum of losses (profits) and costs incurred to the sum of premiums obtained. This indicator does not include the income from investment activities and is considered a good measure of the condition of insurance companies, as it illustrates their ability to generate profits through appropriate insurance risk management. It is also expressed as a percentage. A score below 100% means that the insurer is making a profit (Hayes, 2024; Hayes, 2020). Between 2009 and 2018, the average *loss ratio* was 85.4% (84% in 2018) and the *combined ratio* was 97.6% (97% in 2018) (National Association of Insurance Commissioners, 2019, p. 2). This means that most premium revenues are spent to pay claims. Over the last few years, these ratios have remained stable and at a relatively low level, as well as the profitability of sales.

Fourthly, it is also essential to consider the increase in costs which results in an increase in the nominal amount of premiums so that the activities of insurers do not generate losses. According to a report by the National Association of Insurance Commissioners (NAIC), in 2018 alone, total hospital and medical expenses of insurers increased by more than $28 billion,[24] and administrative expenses increased by another $14 billion.[25] However, the nominal increase in premiums and the increase in premium revenues do not translate into a significantly higher return on sales, which means that, for insurers, increasing the amount of premiums serves more to maintain the profitability of the business than to increase profits. This is not a new phenomenon. Based on the financial results of the largest health insurers in the USA (made available in the Fortune 500), some interesting observations can be made.

Fifthly, the profitability of the most efficient representatives of the industry is quite diverse in relation to one other and sometimes higher than the market average of previous years. However, this should not come as a surprise, as these entities are the best at managing risk. Secondly, despite this, their return on sales results is still relatively lower than the median for the entire Fortune 500. Thirdly, while the median return on sales for the entire ranking has remained the same over the years (7.6–7.44%), it has decreased from 4.9% to 3% in the case of health insurers. Fourthly, in 2019 only in 2 out of 8 cases the increase in profits was higher than the increase in revenues (in percentage), which indicates, among other things, problems with rising costs. Fifthly, Cigna – the insurer with the highest return on sales in 2019 (5.42%) – was still significantly different from the median for the entire ranking (7.44%) (Tables 2.4 and 2.5).

Table 2.4 Financial performance of the highest revenue health insurers 2019 according to the Fortune 500

		Year: 2019			
		Revenue		*Profits*	
Company	*Profitability of sales (%)*	*$ mln*	*Change in revenues since 2018 (%)*	*$ mln*	*Change in profits since 2018 (%)*
UnitedHealth Group	5,30	226 247	12,5	11 986	13,5
Anthem	4,08	92 015	2,3	3 750	−2,4
Centene	1,50	60 116	23,8	900	8,7
Humana	3,00	56 192	5,8	1 683	31,3
Cigna	5,42	48 650	16,9	2 637	17,9
WellCare Health Plans	2,15	20 414	20	440	17,7
Molina Healthcare	3,74	18 890	−5	707	n.d.
Magellan Health	0,33	7 314	25,3	24	−78,1
Triple-S Management	−2,11	2 996,1	2,7	−63	−216,2
Median	**3**				
Fortune 500 median	**7,44**				

Source: Own study based on: Fortune, n.d.

The erosion of private insurance and the future of the U.S. health care system

It can be stated that the contemporary picture of the health insurance market and the way insurers operate deviates from market conditions. Insurers cannot provide adequate services in their main market, so they are looking for alternative solutions on the market of new technologies or government health programmes. However, despite the existing problems, the health insurance market still plays an important, if not crucial, role in the American health care system. Although this position does not result from unfettered market processes, further weakening of insurers will only worsen the situation. The private health insurance market, despite its problems, is one of the main barriers to the introduction of mandatory government insurance for all Americans. Proponents of this idea must consider not only the resistance of institutions such as the AMA, which already opposed such plans in the past, but also the obstacle of the health insurance market, including self-financing plans. A single-payer system would severely restrict this market, which would mean depriving workers of

Table 2.5 Financial performance of the highest revenue health insurers in 2007 according to the Fortune 500

		Year: 2007			
		Revenue		*Profits*	
Company	*Profitability of sales (%)*	*$ mln*	*Change in revenues since 2005 (%)*	*$ mln*	*Change in profits since 2005 (%)*
UnitedHealth Group	5,81	71 542	58	4 159	26
Wellpoint	5,43	56 953	26	3 095	26
Aetna	6,66	25 569	12	1 702	4
Humana	2,27	21 417	49	487	58
Cigna	6,98	16 547	−1	1 155	−29
Health Net	2,55	12 908	8	329	43
Coventry Health Care	7,24	7 734	17	560	12
WellCare Health Plans	3,69	3 763	100	139	168
Amerigroup	3,77	2 835	22	107	100
Centene	−1,93	2 279	51	−44	−178
Medical Mutual of Ohio	4,90	2 039	10	100	57
Molina Healthcare	2,29	2 005	22	46	66
Sierra Health Services	8,14	1 719	24	140	17
Median	**4,9**				
Fortune 500 median	**7,6**				

Source: own study based on: CNN Money, n.d.

access to medical services, tax benefits, etc. Such reasoning also leads to the conclusion that any intervention that destabilizes this market is another (conscious or not) step on the way to the introduction of this system.

Importantly, such interventions do not have to eliminate market institutions directly but may lead to it indirectly by gradually making the principles of their operation similar to non-market solutions. This is exactly the process that is taking place in the private health insurance market. State regulations interfere with the risk assessment process and determine what is to be insured. Insurers are increasingly interested in servicing government health programmes. As a result, market institutions and their offerings become similar to government health programmes, where risk calculation or competition processes do not occur. This kind of erosion of the private health insurance market and insurance institutions is blurring the differences between market-based and interventionist products.

This can be seen, for example, in the increase in costs in both government and private insurance. This is well illustrated by Figure 2.11 which compares the average increase in spending per beneficiary in Medicare and private health insurance. The dynamics of cost growth are very similar, except for the years 2010–2018, when the pace of Medicare spending slowed due to cuts and the influx of younger (less expensive) beneficiaries of the programme. However, according to estimates for the period 2018–2028, these values will again be very close to each other (Cubansky, Neuman & Freed, 2019). Despite the different groups of beneficiaries, these similar results should not be surprising – mainly due to the many interventions carried out in the past.

The above data also demonstrates that insurers and employers can take action to slow or stop cost increases, such as provide services within a given network, telemedicine, and programmes rewarding a healthy lifestyle of employees. However, they will not lead to a decrease in costs (or an increase below the CPI). This is not proof of the flaws of the market, but of the effectiveness of interventionism understood in the sense that compliance with given regulations, from the economic point of view, must lead to an increase in costs. Nevertheless, it does not have to be this way. The development of the cosmetic surgery market, retail clinic chains or medical tourism shows that these costs can be much lower, and their level can be consistently reduced by market competition processes operating away from the regulations covering so many areas of the American health care system.

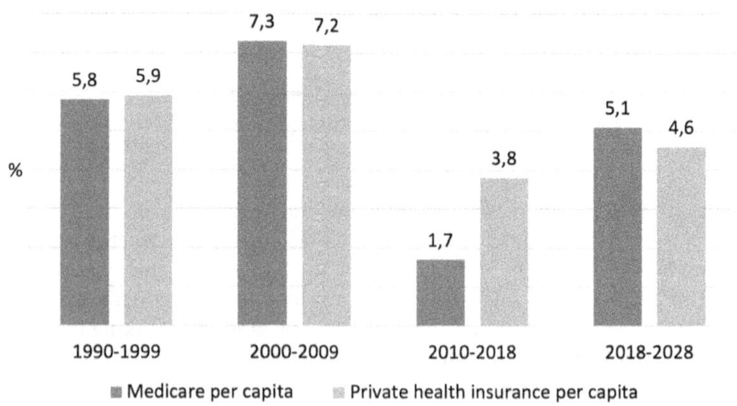

Figure 2.11 Average annual percentage increase in per capita expenditure on Medicare and private health insurance (PHI) by period.

Source: Own study based on: Cubansky, Neuman & Freed, 2019.

Note: The estimates for PHI cover the period 2018–2027.

Notes

1 This form of insurance should not be confused with private individual (non-group) health insurance concluded without the participation of the employer, which in 2018 covered over 19 million people (7% of the US population).
2 An increase in contributions also took place in the 1990s and 1980s. For example, the average of employers' spending on health care between 1985 and 1990 was 11.3%, falling to 6.3% in the 1990s. The percentage increase in premiums in the 1990s (on an annual basis) was as follows: 1991 (11.5%), 1992 (10.9%), 1993 (8%), 1994 (4.8%), 1995 (2.1%), 1996 (0.5%), 1997 (no data), 1998 (3.7%), 1999 (4.1%). Some attribute this decline to the introduction of managed care plans, which reduced patient and physician autonomy to reduce costs. However, at the beginning of the 21st century, premiums began to increase again by several percent. See: Kovner & Jonas, 2002, p. 445; Gabel et al., 2003, pp. 118–119.
3 People 18-64 years old.
4 In 2018, 70% of uninsured employees worked for companies that did not offer health insurance.
5 Employing more than 200 employees.
6 In 2009 it was 65%.
7 This solution operates in a similar way to, for example, exemption from income tax and tax on salaries, on contributions paid by employers and tax reliefs to which employees are entitled.
8 In addition, the sum of the deductible, coinsurance and copayment for these plans cannot exceed $6,900 (individual option) and $13,800 (family option) during the year. These costs can only be higher if one pays for services outside the network.
9 Plans with an HSA account offered by 26% of all companies are much more popular compared to HRAs offered by 4% of companies (both plans can be offered by the same company).
10 23% of them were enrolled in HSA plans, and 7% in HRA.
11 For more, see: Department of The Treasury, 2020, p. 40.
12 For more, see: Department of The Treasury, 2018, pp. 25–26.
13 $2,9 billion out of $3,3 billion.
14 Those employing fewer than 50 employees.
15 The prices given are likely for 2009, when SCO decided to publish their prices for over 100 surgeries.
16 The price of SCO is the total cost.
17 Thus, it was not self-insurance.
18 For more, see: Brook, H. L. et al., 2006.
19 For example, in the US, a knee replacement for one employee would cost more than $50,000. In Costa Rica, the cost was about half of that amount. The cost of gastric surgery (in the case of another employee) would be $30,000, but in Costa Rica it is already just over half of this amount. In addition, employees received a bonus of at least $2,500 – all thanks to the savings. The media also give additional publicity to such stories. For more, see: Pitts & Battiste, 2013.

20 Another example is Dr Azad Moopen who created an international network of medical facilities – Aster DM Healthcare – which includes 16 hospitals, 85 clinics, and about 200 pharmacies operating in the Middle East and India. Over one thousand people are employed in these centres, and the network is constantly developing – new, specialist medical facilities are being established (Sanandaji, 2020, p. 32); Another Indian entrepreneur who has been successful in this field is Dr Ranjan Pai who manages the Manipal Education and Medical Group – a network of 6 universities and 16 hospitals operating in India, Malaysia, Dubai, and Nepal. The network offers a variety of treatments, such as: comprehensive check-ups, cardiac care, spine treatment, cancer treatment, kidney transplantation, or brain surgery (Sanandaji, 2020, pp. 32–33).

21 For more, see: Trefis, n.d.

22 Managed care refers to several activities focused on reducing costs while maintaining the quality of medical services provided under a given insurance programme. Examples of these activities include, e.g., the management and supervision of a network of suppliers.

23 See: Luthra & Greenberg, 2019.

24 An increase by 5% compared to 2017.

25 An increase of 17,7% compared to 2017; National Association of Insurance Commissioners, 2019, p. 1.

References

Aetna (2018). 2018 Notice of Annual Meeting, 2018 Proxy Statement and 2017 Annual Report on Form 10-K, www.annualreports.com/HostedData/AnnualReports/PDF/NYSE_AET_2017.pdf (accessed: 20.10.2024).

Aetna (n.d.). 2009 Aetna Annual Report, Financial Report to Shareholders, www.annualreports.com/HostedData/AnnualReportArchive/a/NYSE_AET_2009.pdf (accessed: 20.10.2024).

Barnett, J. C., & Berchick, E. R. (2017). *Health insurance coverage in the United States: 2016*, Census Bureau.

Brook, H. L. et al. (2006). *The Health Insurance Experiment: A Classic RAND Study Speaks to the Current Health Care Reform Debate*, RAND Corporation.

Claxton, G. et al. (2018). Increases in cost-sharing payments continue to outpace wage growth, www.healthsystemtracker.org/brief/increases-in-cost-sharing-payments-have-far-outpaced-wage-growth/ (accessed: 20.10.2024).

CNN Money (n.d.). Fortune 500 (2007), www.money.cnn.com/magazines/fortune/fortune500/2007/industries/Health_Care_Insurance_Managed_Care/1.html (accessed: 20.10.2024).

Congressional Budget Office (1994). *The Tax Treatment of Employment-Based Health Insurance*. Congressional Budget Office.

Congressional Budget Office (2019a). The Federal Budget in 2018: An Infographic, www.cbo.gov/publication/55342 (accessed: 20.10.2024).

Congressional Budget Office (2019b). Updated Budget Projections: 2019 to 2029, www.cbo.gov/publication/55151 (accessed: 20.10.2024).

Consumers for Quality Care (2018). Consumers Lose When Hospitals and Insurers Agree to Secret Contracts, www.consumers4qualitycare.org/consumers-lose-when-hospitals-and-insurers-agree-to-secret-contracts/ accessed: 20.10.2024).

Cubansky, J., Neuman, T., & Freed, M. (2019). The Facts on Medicare Spending and Financing, www.kff.org/medicare/issue-brief/the-facts-on-medicare-spending-and-financing/ (accessed: 15.04.2020).

Dalen, J. E., & Alpert, J. S. (2019). 'Medical Tourists: Incoming and Outgoing', *The American Journal of Medicine*, *132*: 9–10.

Department of The Treasury (2018). Tax Expenditures: FY2020, https://home.treasury.gov/system/files/131/Tax-Expenditures-FY2020.pdf (accessed: 20.10.2024).

Department of The Treasury (2020). Tax Expenditures: FY2021 (Released February 2020), https://home.treasury.gov/system/files/131/Tax-Expenditures-2021.pdf (accessed: 20.10.2024).

Department Of the Treasury (n.d.). Tax Expenditures, https://home.treasury.gov/policy-issues/tax-policy/tax-expenditures (accessed: 20.10.2024).

DeSimone, N. (2018). Why You're Paying More (and More) For Health Care, www.fee.org/articles/why-you-re-paying-more-and-more-for-health-care/?utm_source=zapier&utm (accessed: 20.10.2024).

Fortune (n.d.). Fortune 500 (2019), www.fortune.com/fortune500/2019/search/?industry=Health%20Care%3A%20Insurance%20and%20Managed%20Care (accessed: 20.10.2024).

Gabel, J. et al. (2003). 'Health Benefits In 2003: Premiums Reach Thirteen-Year High as Employers Adopt New Forms of Cost Sharing', *Health Affairs*, *5*: 118–119.

Galles, G. (2018). Stop Hating on High-Deductible Health Plan, www.mises.org/mises-wire/stop-hating-high-deductible-health-plans (accessed: 20.10.2024).

Getzen, T. E. (2012). *Health Economics and Financing*. Wiley.

Goldberg, S. E., Fragala, M. S., & Wohlgemuth, J. G. (2019). 'Self-Insured Employer Health Benefits Strategy Established a Negative Cost Trend While Improving Performance', *Population Health Management*, *6*: 547–548.

Gottlieb, A. (2016). *The Steadying State of Medicaid in the United States*, PwC.

Hayes, A. (2020). Combined Ratio Definition, www.investopedia.com/terms/c/combinedratio.asp (accessed: 20.10.2024).

Hayes, A. (2024). Loss Ratio, www.investopedia.com/terms/l/loss-ratio.asp (accessed: 20.10.2024)

HealthCare.gov (n.d.). High Deductible Health Plan (HDHP), www.healthcare.gov/glossary/high-deductible-health-plan/ (accessed: 20.10.2024).

Herman, B. (2016). The health insurance industry's identity crisis, www.modernhealthcare.com/article/20160130/MAGAZINE/301309964/the-health-insurance-industry-s-identity-crisis (accessed: 20.10.2024).

Hyman, D. A., & Silver, C. (2018). *Overcharged: Why Americans Pay Too Much For Health Care*, Cato Institute.

Jacobson, G. et al. (2019). A Dozen Facts About Medicare Advantage in 2019, www.kff.org/medicare/issue-brief/a-dozen-facts-about-medicare-advantage-in-2019/ (accessed: 10.04.2020).

Japsen, B. (2019). As Sanders and Warren Attack, Health Insurer Profits Soar, www.forbes.com/sites/brucejapsen/2019/08/04/as-sanders-and-warren-attack-private-health-insurer-profits-soar/#2af55502532b (accessed: 20.10.2024).

Kaiser Family Foundation (2018). 2018 Employer Health Benefits Chart Pack, www.kff.org/slideshow/2018-employer-health-benefits-chart-pack/ (accessed: 19.10.2024).

Kaiser Family Foundation (2019a). *Employer Health Benefits 2019 Annual Survey*. Henry J. Kaiser Family Foundation.

Kaiser Family Foundation (2019b). Medicare Advantage, www.kff.org/medicare/fact-sheet/medicare-advantage/ (accessed: 10.04.2020).

Kaiser Family Foundation (2019c). Premiums and Worker Contributions Among Workers Covered by Employer-Sponsored Coverage, 1999–2019, www.kff.org/interactive/premiums-and-worker-contributions-among-workers-covered-by-employer-sponsored-coverage-1999-2019/#/?compare=true&coverageGroupComp=family (accessed: 19.10.2024).

Kaiser Family Foundation (n.d.). Health Insurance Coverage of Nonelderly 0-64, www.kff.org/other/state-indicator/nonelderly-0-64/?dataView=1&currentTimeframe=0&sortModel=%7B%22colId%22:%22Location%22,%22sort%22:%22asc%22%7D (accessed: 19.10.2024).

Kovner, A. R., & Jonas, S. (2002). *Health Care Delivery in the United States*. Springer Publishing Company.

Luthra, S., & Greenberg, J. (2019). 'Medicare for All' Emerges as Early Divide in First Democratic Debate, www.khn.org/news/medicare-for-all-emerges-as-early-divide-in-first-democratic-debate/ (accessed: 20.10.2024).

Makary, M. (2019). *The Price We Pay: What Broke American Health Care – And How to Fix It*, Bloomsbury Publishing. [Ebook].

National Association of Insurance Commissioners (2019). *U.S. Health Insurance Industry: 2018 Annual Results*, National Association of Insurance Commissioners.

O'Neill, M. (n.d.). Unusual Heart Therapy Wins Coverage from Large Insurer, www.nytimes.com/1993/07/28/health/unusual-heart-therapy-wins-coverage-from-large-insurer.html (accessed: 20.10.2024); A digital version of an article originally published in New York Times on June 28th, 1993.

Patient Beyond Borders (n.d.). Quick facts about medical tourism, www.patientsbeyondborders.com/media (accessed: 08.04.2020).

Pitts, B., & Battiste, N. (2013). As More Americans Have Surgeries Overseas, US Companies Consider 'Medical Tourism' a Health Care Option, www.abcnews.go.com/Health/americans-surgeries-overseas-us-companies-medical-tourism-health/story?id=20423011 (accessed: 20.10.2024).

Pope, C. (2019). Issues 2020: Private Health Insurance Saves Americans Money, www.manhattan-institute.org/issues-2020-health-care-reform-private-insurance#notes (accessed: 20.10.2024).

Quirk, J. (2017). *Seasteading: How Floating Nations Will Restore the Environment, Enrich the Poor, Cure the Sick, and Liberate Humanity from Politicians*. Free Press. [Ebook].

Rae, M., Copeland, R., & Cox, C. (2019). Tracking the Rise In Premium Contributions And Cost-Sharing For Families With Large Employer Coverage, www.healthsystemtracker.org/brief/tracking-the-rise-in-premium-contributions-and-cost-sharing-for-families-with-large-employer-coverage/ (accessed: 20.10.2024).

Sackville, T. (2013). 'Czynniki hamujące rozwój dobrowolnych ubezpieczeń zdrowotnych na rynku brytyjskim' ['Factors inhibiting the development of voluntary health insurance in the UK market'], *Dodatkowe ubezpieczenia zdrowotne. Efektywny system na tle doświadczeń europejskich* [*Supplementary health insurance. An effective system against the background of the European experience*] *4*: 95–99.

Sanandaji, N. (2020). *The Henry Fords of Healthcare*. Institute of Economic Affairs.

Saywer, B., Cox, C., & Claxton G. (2017). An analysis of who is most at risk for high out-of-pocket health spending, www.healthsystemtracker.org/brief/who-is-most-at-risk-for-high-out-of-pocket-health-spending/#item-start (accessed: 20.10.2024).

Self-Insurance Institute of America (n.d.). Self-insured health group plan, www.siia.org/i4a/pages/index.cfm?pageID=4546 (accessed: 10.20.2024).

Tolbert, J. et al. (2019). Key Facts about the Uninsured Population, www.kff.org/uninsured/issue-brief/key-facts-about-the-uninsured-population/ (accessed: 27.03.2020).

Trefis (n.d.). UNH Revenues: How Does UnitedHealth Make Money?, https://dashboards.trefis.com/no-login-required/yiEfzczN/UnitedHealth-Revenues-How-Does-UnitedHealth-Make-Money-?fromforbesandarticle=unh190916 (accessed: 10.04.2020).

UnitedHealth Group (n.d.). Annual Reports & Proxy Statements, www.unitedhealthgroup.com/investors/annual-reports.html (accessed: 10.04.2020).

Wilde Mathews, A. (2018). Behind Your Rising Health-Care Bills: Secret Hospital Deals That Squelch Competition, www.wsj.com/articles/behind-your-rising-health-care-bills-secret-hospital-deals-that-squelch-competition-1537281963 (accessed: 09.04.2020).

Wojcik, J. (2013). Self-insured firms offer medical tourism option to cut health care costs, www.businessinsurance.com/article/00010101/NEWS06/312159991/Self-insured-firms-offer-medical-tourism-option-to-cut-health-care-costs (accessed: 20.10.2024).

3 Public (government) health insurance programmes

Development of market institutions before the introduction of government programmes

At various intervals, there were interventions introduced that had a significant impact on demand factors, not only on supply. In the USA, the first public social security programmes were introduced in 1935 when the Social Security Act (SSA) was passed. Partial or direct state health care had to wait until 1964–1965, when the Medicare and Medicaid programmes were created.[1] Previous attempts to create Mandatory Health Insurance (MHI) along the lines of European countries had failed.

The creation of Medicare and Medicaid had a significant impact on the current structure of financing access to health care in the USA, still dominated by a third party, i.e., an entity (institution) that covers most of the expenses for medical care for the consumer. When a consumer bears most or all the costs of purchasing certain goods and services, they try to act in a rational way so as not to incur unnecessary losses. On the other hand, if it is only a fraction of the costs they incur, they are mainly guided by non-price factors such as quality or availability of services. As a result, the rationality of consuming such services is undermined, and it is more difficult for insurers and service providers to provide access to medical care without increasing their premiums and the cost of services.

Nevertheless, prior to the introduction of these two programmes, there had been many market institutions in the USA that provided the poor and those in need with access to many services, including medical ones. At the turn of the 20th century, the most popular among the working class were *fraternal societies*, institutions of mutual aid. At that time, typical health insurance was not popular among this social class, which does not mean that this part of society was deprived of medical care. By 1920, more than 25% of U.S. adults belonged to these institutions. Members of the associations, in exchange for monthly fees, had access to many services offered: payment of benefits to the family after the death of its member or the occurrence of a disability, or the so-called *lodge practices* which consisted

DOI: 10.4324/9781003588108-4

in concluding agreements between associations and doctors. In exchange for a predetermined fee (instead of a fee for the visit), the doctors provided their services to the members of the association or their families. Contracts were renewed if the quality of the services provided was satisfactory. The cost of these services was relatively low, averaging about \$1–\$2 for each member per year, which was the market cost of a single visit. \$1–\$2 was also equivalent to a day's wages. Such a low cost was the result of two factors. Firstly, doctors competed for contracts with associations because they had stable incomes. Secondly, the members of the associations kept an eye on each other, minimizing the phenomenon of moral hazard, which allowed to keep the premiums at a relatively low level (Starr, 1982, pp. 206–209; Long, n.d.).

In addition to fraternal associations, the so-called *group practices* were developing, associating doctors in one institution. Some of the doctors who contributed capital became the owners of such institutions. The Mayo Clinic can be cited as an example. These institutions offered a high standard of specialized services, but competition and proper management kept prices relatively low. This was met with disapproval by some doctors who complained that the activities of institutions such as the Mayo Clinic led to under-pricing (Starr, 1982, p. 213). Therefore, the AMA made it difficult for doctors to set up these types of institutions.

The AMA also took decisive action against physicians who collaborated with *fraternal societies*, threatening them with expulsion from its structures. This was one of the reasons for the decline of fraternal societies. In addition, the limited supply of doctors increased prices, which made *lodge practices* less financially attractive for their members. Also important were the activities of the National Fraternal Congress, a union of fraternal societies, which lobbied for the introduction of a minimum fee. All these actions led to the lower competitiveness of these institutions and the gradual marginalization of their role in financing access to medical services in the USA (Long, n.d.).

Private health insurance also played a role in this process, and it began to attract more and more interest among the members of the societies. Younger members joined the societies mainly because of the possibility of receiving sickness benefits. Due to their age and the lack of older working children, they did not have the opportunity to join their health insurance (the family option). Initially, they did not have sufficient savings to finance their health expenses in the future either (e.g., because of a disability). At the beginning of the 20th century, the loss of income of the primary breadwinner was a risk for the entire family. Hence, there were many benefits to joining fraternal societies. As the savings of younger members began to grow, their children took up jobs, and the alternatives in the form of self-insurance or family insurance became more attractive since they had lower transaction costs, and the funds were kept in the family. As a result, some members began to resign from participating in lodge practices. However, this did not lead to the disappearance of the societies themselves, as sickness benefits or other medical services offered through them were only part of their wide offer. Other members paid more attention to socio-cultural factors, such as the desire to belong to a given community (Emery & Herbert Emery, 1999, pp. 103, 115–116). As it can be seen, the multiplicity and interchangeability of market solutions in the field of financing access to health services have a positive impact on meeting important social needs.

Another important factor contributing to the development of market institutions was the increasing productivity of American workers, which resulted in higher wages and savings. According to John C. Herbert Emery, relatively high incomes and savings were the main reasons for the rejection of the idea of mandatory health insurance in the USA at the beginning of the 20th century. According to the researcher, it was not the lack of awareness of American workers or the presentation of the concept of mandatory insurance as contrary to American values that was behind its failure, but relatively high wages and growing savings. After all, American values did not help to stop plans to implement the Social Security Act of 1935. Furthermore, Emery points out that states with lower savings rates supported the introduction of MHI, as opposed to states where the rates were higher (Herbert Emery, 2012, pp. 121–136).

In addition to economic factors, the AMA and its initiatives also played a role in the rejection of the MHI. It was then that less ambitious, but more likely to succeed, solutions were considered. Such solutions include the idea of creating a programme informally called *federal hospital insurance*, which would cover the elderly (over 65). In 1952, President Harry Truman appointed a committee that published a report recommending a more modest federally funded and state-administered programme. The guidelines in the report later became the basis for the Medicare programme signed into law by President Lyndon Johnson in 1965 (Doherty & Jenkins, 2009, pp. 19–20).

Reasons for the enactment of Medicare and Medicaid

The introduction of Medicare was not only the result of the political will to create such a programme but was also a consequence of previous interventions in the market. In addition to private health insurance and fraternal societies, from the late 1930s, alternatives were developing in the form of Blue Shield/Blue Cross health plans. Commercial insurance based on risk assessment had procedures including, for example, the payment of benefits or the financing of hospital stays. These regulations also applied to doctors, who, opposing this type of practice, began to create their own insurance plans (Blue Shield) in which their activities were not so strongly controlled. At the same time, in 1939, on the initiative of the American Hospital Association (AHA), other insurance plans (Blue Cross) were created to finance the insured's stay in the hospital. Blue Shield and Blue Cross (also known as Blues) were intended to provide an alternative to traditional commercial insurance which, according to many doctors, limited patients' access to medical services to some extent. However, the restrictions applied by insurers are designed to keep premiums at an appropriate level, which guarantees the stability of the insurance programme. In addition, not all medical procedures may be covered by health insurance.

To consolidate their position in the market, the Blues sought the support of state governments. These efforts were successful and these institutions, unlike their competitors, received many privileges: exemption from taxes paid on the premiums collected, and lower requirements for maintaining reserves to cover their liabilities. However, in exchange for these privileges, the state authorities required the use of a calculation of premiums based not on insurance risk but on uniform criteria for all the insured people (*community rating*), which, as it later turned out, had very far-reaching consequences. State government support contributed to the growing popularity of these health plans, mistakenly equated with insurance. An additional factor influencing the growth of their popularity was the uncertainty that came with the Great Depression and the support of the AMA. Thanks to these solutions, doctors could count on stable employment and salaries, and their clients could count on programmes that were competitively priced and had a wider range than insurance itself. These factors led to Blue Shield/Blue Cross achieving a dominant position in the industry. In 1950, Blue Shield had a 52% market share of standard medical insurance and Blue Cross had a 49% share of the hospital insurance market. These institutions merged in 1982, and by the beginning of the 21st century, one in three Americans used them (McGuff & Murphy, 2015, pp. 20–21; Steinreich 2004).

Although Blue Shield and Blue Cross are referred to as insurance, the rules on which these institutions operate differ from those used by real insurers. Steinreich (2004) points out four important differences between the two:

- Hospitals were paid on a cost-plus basis. Insurers were paid not a sum of prices charged to patients for certain services but costs that bore no necessary relationship to prices for services performed.
- Insurance of even routine procedures. This spelled the end of true insurance. What replaced it was not actual insurance but prepaid consumption that encouraged overuse of services.
- Insurance premiums based on "community rating." The word "community" meant that every person in a specific geographic area

regardless of age, habits, occupation, race, or sex was charged the same price. For example, the average 60-year-old incurs four times the medical expense of the average 25-year-old, but under community rating both are charged the same price, which is another way of saying that young people are overcharged and the elderly undercharged.
- Pay-as-you-go system. Unlike the sound type of hospital insurance which placed premiums in growing reserves to pay claims, "insurance" created by the Blues collected premiums that only covered the expected costs incurred by policy holders over the following year. If a large group of policyholders became ill over the course of several years, the premiums of all policyholders had to be raised to cover the increase in costs.

Insurers who wanted to compete with the Blues, at least partially, had to make their offer similar and seek support from the legislator. A good opportunity to do so was the wage freeze in the USA during World War II. Unable to offer higher wages to employees, companies began to offer them health insurance as non-wage employee benefits which were not covered by the regulations. The premiums paid by the employees could be deducted from the tax base. As a result, more and more Americans were gaining access to medical services through employee health insurance and the Blues.

However, the principles on which the Blue Cross/Blue Shield health plans operated differed significantly from the activities of insurers. The same premium for all participants led to an increase in costs, which was a growing problem for the institutions themselves and for the younger insured people who could afford to leave the programme.[2] The problem was solved not by abolishing the previous regulations but by introducing new ones. Some of the insured (65 and older) were to switch to government insurance, i.e., the Medicare programme. This was beneficial for the Blues, because (at the taxpayer's expense) they got rid of the insured generating the highest and constantly growing costs. For politicians, on the other hand, it was a good opportunity to show that the government took care of the problem. An additional advantage of this solution was the implementation, after many years of efforts, of government health insurance.

The problems faced by private institutions were not due to market failure, but to previous government interventions in their sphere of activity. Although these interventions initially seemed insignificant and very beneficial to both sides, over time they became the cause of serious problems. Market institutions did not compete for customers using methods characteristic of a market economy, but thanks to the privileges received from the state. This led to a situation in which these institutions increasingly resembled income redistribution programmes between younger and older insured people, i.e., solutions characteristic of public health systems. In the conditions of an unfettered market economy, the elderly could take advantage of many alternative solutions, such as: previously collected savings, family support, and charitable activities carried out by many non-profit institutions. Also, the Blues would be forced to manage more effectively without government support. Processes of competition between them, insurers, fraternal societies, group practice institutions, and other charitable organizations would create a *bottom-up safety net*. The economic contribution of older people to the economy would be appropriately used for their future health needs. Under such conditions, the growing needs of the elderly would not be the cost and problem they are now for government insurance, but, in a sense, they would be the consumption of specific goods from their previous *investments*. Instead, it was decided to postpone the problem and, in fact, to pass the costs on to the rest of society. The main problem was that the Medicare programme, like the Blues, operated under the four guidelines above, which after a few decades led to similar negative effects that are now visible across the whole country.

Characteristics of Medicare

The solutions on which the Medicare programme (and Medicaid) was based in the first two decades of its operation led to a crisis and subsequent interventions in the 1980s. It is essential to consider the intentions of the originators of these programmes to better understand the problems and their current shape.

Originally, it was assumed that Medicare would only cover Hospital Insurance (HI) Part A of Medicare. However, Willbur Mills, who led the work on Medicare implementation, feared that the scope of services would be too modest, which would cause public discontent and pressure to expand it. This, in turn, would lead to an increase in payroll taxes from which Part A was to be financed. Therefore, an alternative plan previously created by Republicans, which now functions as Supplementary Medical Insurance (SMI) – also known as Part B, was included in the programme. Part B is voluntary and is funded from sources other than Part A: premiums from beneficiaries and from the Department of Finance's general fund. The Medicare programme was only meant to be a stopover on the road to creating universal health insurance that would eventually cover all Americans. Although these issues were not officially raised in the debate preceding the introduction of Medicare, these were the intentions of its creators. For the originators of Medicare, the initial version of the programme covering the elderly was feasible (politically viable) as opposed to universal health insurance. According to the creators' assumptions, over time, more social groups (children, employees, etc.) were to be included in Medicare.[3] Mills, who feared such a scenario, added a proposal for an additional programme (Medicaid) to cover people with lower incomes. Through separate government insurance, Mills wanted to weaken the case for expanding Medicare in the future. Thus, the limited scope of Medicare (Part A) was expanded to include Part B and separate Medicaid insurance (Marmor & Oberlander, 2016, pp. 744–747).

Currently, Medicare consists of four parts:

1 Part A includes hospital insurance providing access to, among other things, hospital services, home treatment, and hospice stays. Part A is funded primarily by the Federal Insurance Contributions Act (FICA). The tax is 2.9% of earnings and is paid by the employee and the employer (1.45% by each party). In 2018, 88% of Part A was financed by payroll tax revenues. Taxpayers with higher incomes (more than $200,000 per person and $250,000 per couple) pay a higher tax rate of 2.35%. Beneficiaries are also required to cover part of the cost of hospital services.
2 Part B is voluntary medical insurance covering the cost of outpatient services, which is financed mainly by the general fund of the Department of Finance (72%) and by premiums from beneficiaries (26%). Currently, Part B, along with the later created Part D, make up Supplementary Medical Insurance (SMI). Again, the beneficiaries cover part of the cost of outpatient services.
3 Part C, otherwise known as Medicare Advantage, is an alternative form of receiving benefits under Medicare. Normally, healthcare providers under Parts A and B are paid for each service they provide (*fee for service*). Under Medicare Advantage, policyholders can choose other forms of medical services, such as Health Maintenance Organization (HMO) or Preferred Provider Organizations (PPO). The Medicare Advantage (Part C) programme is not separately funded. Medicare Advantage plans, such as HMOs and PPOs, include Part A, Part B, and (usually) Part D. Medicare Advantage plan beneficiaries pay a Part B premium and pay an additional premium if their plan requires it.
4 Individuals who use Part A or B may also participate in the subsidized access to Prescription Drug Insurance Programme for an additional premium. Part D is mainly financed by the Department of Finance's general fund (71%) and by beneficiary premiums (17%) (Folland, Goodman & Stano, 2013, pp. 440–445; Cubansky, Neuman & Freed, 2019).

Medicare financing costs

The sources of the problems and negative effects of the Medicare programme can be found, among other things, in the way it was financed. This programme, as mentioned earlier, operated based on four main assumptions, which significantly differed from the principles of real insurance companies.

Medicare evolved in several stages. The first was from the mid-1960s to the mid-1980s when Medicare financed access to medical services on a cost-plus basis. Previously, the BlueShield/Blue Cross programmes had already been operating on this basis. In the cost-plus system, the payer (Medicare) covers the cost of all services provided by providers (e.g., hospitals) to the insured. It was a very advantageous situation for the providers, as the bill for each service provided was covered by the payer, and only a small part of it was covered by the insured. The funds at the taxpayer's disposal come mostly from taxes, and the share of premiums paid by the insured is relatively small. As a result, neither side has sufficient economic incentives to control the costs of scarce resources. Suppliers set their costs separately from existing prices, as this increases their profits. In addition, doctors were not limited in the number of examinations or consultations they performed, and their limitations resulted more from the observance of the Hippocratic Oath than from economic calculation. Acquiring new and expensive technologies is also not a problem either, as in the end most of the costs were borne by taxpayers. It can even be concluded that it was profitable for the suppliers (Goodman & Musgrave, 1992, pp. 21–23).

Today, technology is mistakenly considered to be one of the reasons for rising costs in healthcare. The increasing number of people insured by Medicare has also gradually contributed to the marginalization of the share of direct payments in financing access to medical services. Therefore, the cost-plus system had to lead to a rapid escalation of costs. As Theodore Marmor and Jonathan Oberlander (2016, pp. 749–750) point out:

> In the first year of Medicare's operation, the average daily service charge in American hospitals increased by an unprecedented 21.9 percent.21 The average compound rate of growth in this figure over the next five years was 13 percent. Medicare's definition of "reasonable charges" paved the way for steep increases in physician fees. In the eleven months between the time Medicare was enacted and the time it took effect, the rate of increase in physician fees more than doubled, from 3.8 percent in 1965 to 7.8 percent in 1966. The average compound rate of growth in physician fees remained a high 6.8 percent over the next five years. In the first five full years of Medicare's operation, total Medicare reimbursements rose 72 percent, from $4.6 billion in 1967 to $7.9 billion in 1971. Over the same period, the number of Medicare enrollees rose only 6 percent, from 19.5 million in 1967 to 20.7 million in 1971.

The rapidly rising cost of services meant that plans to expand Medicare to include other social groups had to be postponed. However, in the following years, services continued to become more expensive, and the costs of the programme incurred by taxpayers increased. According to Thomas DiLorenzo (2009):

> In 1970 the government forecast that the hospital insurance (HI) portion of Medicare would be "only" $2.9 billion annually. Since the actual expenditures were $5.3 billion, this was a 79 percent underestimate of cost. In 1980 the government forecast $5.5 billion in HI expenditures; actual expenditures were more than four times that amount – $25.6 billion. This bureaucratic cost explosion led the government to enact 23 new taxes in the first 30 years of Medicare.[4]

These data show that Medicare has always been a very unstable programme. Any private entity to overestimate its profit and loss account so much would go out of business very quickly. This is a positive market signal informing the public that scarce resources have been misused. However, there is no profit-and-loss mechanism in the government programme. The increase in costs in the early years of Medicare is even more surprising given that people aged 65 and older and people with disabilities were enrolled, and the average life expectancy in 1966 was just over 70 (66.7 for men and 73.8 for women), which means that increasing life expectancy did not burden Medicare finances as much as it does today. Furthermore, rising costs also began to affect insurance companies and individual buyers, as they also used the services offered by hospitals or doctors – this problem only intensified in the following decades. Rapidly rising costs were also a result of the fact that the originators of Medicare, in the early years of its implementation, were not willing to negotiate harder with providers about the cost of their services, because they wanted good cooperation between all parties. Protracted negotiations with providers could jeopardize the achievement of political goals and the launch of Medicare (Marmor & Oberlander, 2016, p. 750).

However, no government programme can ignore the laws of economics, and again, cost control was only a matter of time in this case as well. In 1983, payments to providers on a cost-plus basis were discontinued, and Diagnostically Related Grouping (DRG) was used to finance treatment. The DRG is a reimbursement system in which payments are made based on homogeneous illness cases. Such grouping of patients is also used to standardize medical services and reduce costs among providers. The problem, however, was that the reality differed from the assumptions made in the DRG model. It was believed that despite the differences between patients, it was possible to successfully apply homogeneous methods of treatment to them, which was also a means to obtain more rational expenses. However, the situation was more complicated, especially among patients with several conditions. Economic aspects were not considered in these activities either. Providers, whose supply had been artificially limited due to previous interventions because of receiving lower revenues (from Medicare and Medicaid) than before, gradually began to pass on the costs to other payers (private insurers) and their customers. They did it because they were not afraid of competition. As a result, reductions in government spending led to an increase in the price of private health insurance, making it less affordable for some Americans. The misidentification of the problem further contributed to the problem, which was thought to be unlimited payment to suppliers for every service paid, while the real problem has been the fact that suppliers did and do not operate under market conditions.

Moreover, the new regulations led to the fact that private insurance companies also started to apply similar restrictions, which resulted in limiting hospital services and developing those areas where they were not so burdensome (e.g., outpatient care). Predetermined payments were, therefore, a specific form of price control imposed on suppliers. Interestingly, limiting spending for suppliers was more beneficial to the government than the regulations directly affecting policyholders.[5] These measures, while politically viable, did not stop the rise in healthcare costs and led to further interventions.

In addition to hospital services, in the early 1990s outpatient care regulations called Evaluation and Management (E&M) also appeared. This intervention had a similar objective to the DRG and consisted of payment for services rendered based on pre-established guidelines. The E&M coding system defines billing levels from the simplest (Level I) to the most complex one (Level V). To bill a higher amount, one needs to collect more data in each lower segment of the medical record. This is more burdensome in the case of more difficult cases, where the speed of action is important. Filling out the proper paperwork takes more time for doctors, which means that they pay less attention to patients. This increase in bureaucracy was aimed at limiting the funds spent – it was hoped that some of the documentation would show that there were no grounds for spending additional funds (McGuff & Murphy, 2015, p. 32–34). The result, however, is a significantly increasing number of administrative staff, especially in the early 1990s, when E&M was introduced, and a few years after the DRG system came into force. From 1975 to 2010, the number of doctors increased by 150%, while the number of administrative staff increased by as much as 3200% over the same period (Cantlupe, 2017).

The issue of relatively low Medicare administrative costs

The belief in the effectiveness of regulation in reducing costs is also reflected in proposals to introduce national health insurance for all Americans (e.g., Medicare for All). The proponents of this solution argue that Medicare has lower administrative costs compared to private health insurance. However, Medicare's advantage in this area is not due to greater efficiency or better management, but to statistics. The beneficiaries of Medicare are the elderly or the disabled, who generate much higher costs of benefits per person than beneficiaries of private health insurance. Administrative costs expressed as a percentage of the (higher) total costs[6] are therefore lower than in private insurance. It is also important to note that in the case of private insurance, this amount is calculated as the difference between the sum of premiums collected and the sum of payments. As a result, costs that are not actually administrative are also recognised as administrative ones, for example, services addressed to patients with chronic diseases or telephone consultations. Because they do not result in direct payment of claims automatically, they are classified as administrative costs and artificially inflate them. Another example of administrative costs is state premium taxes levied on health insurers that are not paid. However, even with these differences, the administrative costs (expressed in American dollars) generated by Medicare were still higher than those of private insurance. For example, in 2000–2005, the administrative costs of Medicare per beneficiary were higher than the costs of private insurance by up to several dozen percent (48.4% in 2000), as shown in Table 3.1.

On the other hand, these costs, expressed as a percentage of total costs, are lower in the case of Medicare mainly because the benefits in these two types of programmes are several times higher. For example, Medicare's administrative costs (in 2005) expressed as a fraction of total costs (per beneficiary) were 5.8% compared to 13.2% for private insurance, which leads to misconceptions about the effectiveness of Medicare. This is because the total costs per beneficiary were more than $8,000 for Medicare and more than $3,000 for private insurance (Book, 2009).

Some of Medicare's administrative costs do not need to be included in these comparisons because they appear in the budgets of other agencies. For instance, the Social Security Administration administers Medicare premiums, and the Internal Revenue Service (IRS) collects taxes. Therefore, Medicare cost estimates may be underestimated (e.g., 3% is given instead of 6%). In addition, fraud is a big problem for Medicare, which also negatively affects comparisons with private insurance. If Medicare devotes less resources to reducing fraud, these costs are treated as medical costs, which at the same time improves the percentage of administrative costs. Meanwhile, when private insurers try to fight fraud, the same rate increases despite the savings that such actions bring (Galles, 2018).

Table 3.1 Comparison of administrative costs of Medicare and private health insurance in 2000–2005

Year	*Medicare*			*Private insurance*			*Percentage difference showing how much higher Medicare costs are*
	Number of beneficiaries (mln.)	*Total administrative costs/expenditure ($ billions)*	*Total administrative costs/expenditure per capita ($)*	*Number of beneficiaries (mln.)*	*Total administrative costs/ expenditure ($ billions)*	*Total administrative costs/expenditure per capita ($)*	
2000	37,06	14,1	380	202,8	52,0	256	48,4%
2001	37,32	14,40	386	201,7	56,6	281	37,5%
2002	37,68	15,84	420	200,9	68,8	342	22,7%
2003	38,11	16,5	433	199,9	82,2	411	5,3%
2004	38,64	20,14	521	200,9	85,3	425	22,7%
2005	39,21	19,94	509	201,2	91,1	453	12,3%

Source: Own study based on: Book, 2009.

Is technology in fact driving costs up in healthcare?

The events described above reflect the expansive nature of interventionism. Successive interventions aimed at solving problems only exacerbate them, leading to further interventions, which increases the participation of the state in a given sector of the economy. Interventions that artificially stimulate demand, leading to an increase in prices rather than an increase in the supply of medical services, are of particular importance. As a result, medical services that were supposed to be more accessible to the public are becoming more and more expensive. Moreover, most of the population, paying only a fraction of the cost, does not directly experience the constant increase in the price of services and is unable to determine their true costs. Households pay only a small fraction of the cost of Medicare, which leads to the illusion of high availability of medical services despite ever-increasing costs. Furthermore, Americans are unable to estimate how much they spend on such expenses out of their own pockets. Government intervention leads to a situation where the most expensive services may seem to be the cheapest. For instance, in the early 1990s Americans spent an average of 4.5%s (out of $1) out of pocket on hospital care, but 68 cents on medicines. Thus, for patients, hospital therapy seems cheaper than pharmacotherapy, when in fact it is the opposite (Robbins, Robbins & Goodman, 1993).

The lack of appropriate economic constraints leads to greater, but not necessarily justified, consumption. Research by Merrill Matthews and Mark Littow, conducted on relatively homogeneous groups in terms of health or age, showed that people qualified for the Medicare programme use medical services about 50% more often than people with private health insurance (Pettegrew, Vance, 2013). Thus, insurances such as Medicare are attractive not only for people who are already ill, but also for people looking for opportunities to increase consumption because of the low price (compared to the benefits obtained) that they would have to pay in the process. This artificially stimulated demand also leads to suppliers (e.g., hospitals) being much more willing to buy new technologies. Patients, paying only a fraction of the cost, have no hesitation to use them on a scale that would be impossible in the case of direct expenses (Finkelstein, 2014, pp. 73–64, 82–83).

In addition, new technologies are making the offer of suppliers even more attractive. Even those suppliers who have not been planning to purchase new technologies need to change their approach, or they may lose some customers. Such conditions lead to a kind of technological arms race between suppliers, which is possible due to the dominant role of third-party payers. This creates additional problems in the form of overconsumption of medical services and higher costs, for example, for people who want to purchase them directly or for charitable institutions. Such situations have led some observers to conclude that it is technology that is behind the ever-increasing costs in healthcare. In fact, every other sector of the economy would develop the same if consumers paid only a fraction of the cost and the main burden was passed on to the rest of society. In this respect, the healthcare sector is no different from the automotive or computer industries.

A different view of the problem is held by William J. Baumol who attributes the increase in prices (above the inflation rate) of such personal services as health care or education to the fact that in these cases it is not easy to reduce the amount of human labour and replace it with more efficient tools or machines. In his opinion, the limited possibilities of automating production processes (in contrast to other sectors of the economy) are responsible for the relatively higher costs of these services and their growing share of expenditure in the economy (Baumol, 2012, pp. XVII–XVIII). Currently, it is still difficult to replace the services provided by doctors (e.g., during surgery) directly and on a mass scale with robots, but new technologies are also being created and developed in medicine to indirectly support medical staff. In this context, it is worth considering how an unfettered market for medical services could function. In the USA, one of the few areas of broadly understood medical services where market processes are not yet constrained by dozens of regulations is the cosmetic surgery market. As it turns out, there are no supply constraints or high price growth rates exceeding the inflation rate in this market. An interesting observation is provided by Mark J. Perry of the American Enterprise Institute, who analysed a 2016 report prepared for the American Society for Aesthetic Plastic Surgery. Perry (2017) pointed out a few facts that show the possibilities of an unfettered market in providing consumers with the goods and services they need:

1 Between 1998 and 2016, the average increase in the prices of the twenty most popular cosmetic surgery procedures was 32%, while the prices of medical care services increased by 100.5%, the prices of hospital services by as much as 176.6%, and the consumer price index (CPI) by 47.2%.
2 For the ten most popular treatments in 2016, none of them have increased their price by more than 47.2% since 1998 (the same as the base inflation rate), which means that the true, inflation-adjusted price of all ten treatments has fallen over the past 18 years.
3 For the three most popular treatments (Botox injection, laser hair removal and chemical peel), prices fell by 11.3%, 21.7% and 34.8%, respectively.
4 The total number of these procedures increased from 660,269 in 1998 to 6,249,894 in 2016.

5 The prices of the two most popular cosmetic surgical procedures in 2016, liposuction and breast augmentation, have increased by 30.6% and 26.2% respectively since 1998. However, both increases were lower than the CPI index in this period (47.2%).
6 The number of all 20 procedures increased from 2,104,674 in 1998 to 8,588,625 in 2016.

Goodman, Musgrave & Herrick (2004, p. 138) point to several reasons for this:

> Despite the quadrupling of the number of surgeries, cosmetic surgeons' fees remained relatively stable. What explains this price stability? One reason is patient behavior. When patients pay with their own money, they have an incentive to be savvy consumers. A second reason is supply. As more people demanded the procedures, more surgeons began to provide them. Since almost any licensed medical doctor may obtain training and perform cosmetic procedures, entry into the field is relatively easy. A third reason is efficiency. Many providers have operating facilities located in their offices, a less expensive alternative to outpatient surgery at a hospital. Surgeons generally adjust their fees to stay competitive and usually quote patients a package price. Absent are the gatekeepers, prior authorization and large medical office billing staffs needed when third-party insurance pays the fees. A fourth reason is the emergence of substitute products.

Thus, competition for customers and consumer independence in the choice of goods and services do not lead to an increase in prices, but to a decrease in prices and better availability. Unfortunately, a significant part of the medical services sector is still heavily regulated – hence, among other things, the constantly rising prices. Also, in cosmetic surgery services it is not possible to completely replace medical staff, but this is not an obstacle to falling prices. It is also worth noting that these types of services are not funded by third-party payers.

Notes

1 Medicare funds access to health care for people over 65. Medicaid, in turn, is responsible for financing such access for the poor. In this part, most attention will be paid to these two programmes due to the significant costs they generate, among other things.
2 It is the so-called affordability spiral.
3 Therefore, there is no coincidence in the recurring ideas of creating government insurance covering all Americans postulated under the slogan *Medicare for all* which are propagated by such representatives of Democrats as Berni Sanders, among others.

4 For more, see: Hamowy, 2000, pp. 15–86.
5 For more, see: Bast, Rue & Wesbury, 1993.
6 Which constitute a sum of administrative costs and payment for services.

References

Bast, J. L., Rue, R. C., & Wesbury, S. (1993). *Why We Spend Too Much on Health Care*, University Press of America.

Baumol, W. J. (2012). *The Cost Disease: Why Computers Get Cheaper and Health Care Doesn't*, Yale University Press.

Book, R. A. (2009). Medicare Administrative Costs Are Higher, Not Lower, Than for Private Insurance, www.heritage.org/health-care-reform/report/medicare-administrative-costs-are-higher-not-lower-private-insurance (accessed: 22.10.2024).

Cantlupe, J. (2017). The rise (and rise) of the healthcare administrator, www.athenahealth.com/insight/expert-forum-rise-and-rise-healthcare-administrator (accessed: 22.10.2024).

Cubansky, J., Neuman, T., & Freed, M. (2019). The Facts on Medicare Spending and Financing, www.kff.org/medicare/issue-brief/the-facts-on-medicare-spending-and-financing/ (accessed: 15.04.2020).

DiLorenzo, T. (2009). Socialized Healthcare vs. The Laws of Economics, www.mises.org/mises-daily/socialized-healthcare-vs-laws-economics (accesses: 22.10.2024).

Doherty, K., & Jenkins, J. A. (2009). Examining a Failed Moment: National Health Care, the AMA, and the U.S. Congress, 1948–50, Paper prepared for the purposes of a presentation given at: "*2009 Annual Meeting of the Southern Political Science Association*".

Emery, G., & Herbert Emery, J. C. (1999). *A Young Man's Benefit. The Independent Order of Odd Fellows and Sickness Insurance in the United States and Canada, 1860–1929*, McGill-Queen's University Press.

Finkelstein, A. (2014). *Moral Hazard in Health Insurance*. Columbia University Press. [Ebook].

Folland, S., Goodman, A. C., & Stano, M. (2013). *The Economics of Health and Health Care* (7th ed.). Pearson.

Galles, G. (2018). Medicare for All: Administrative Costs Are Much Higher than You Think, www.mises.org/wire/medicare-all-administrative-costs-are-much-higher-you-think (accessed: 22.10.2024).

Goodman, J. C., & Musgrave, G. L. (1992). *Patient power. Solving America's health care crisis*, Cato Institute.

Goodman, J. C., Musgrave, G. L., & Herrick D. M. (2004). *Lives at Risk. Single-Payer National Health Insurance around the World*. Rowman & Littlefield Publishers.

Hamowy, R. (2000). The Genesis and Development of Medicare. In R. Feldman (Ed.), *American Health Care*. Independent Institute, pp. 15–86.

Herbert Emery, J. C. (2012). America's Rejection of Government Health Insurance in the Progressive Era: Implications for Understanding the

Determinants and Achievements of Public Insurance of Health Risks. In B. Harris (Ed.), *Welfare and Old Age in Europe and North America*. Routledge, pp. 121–136.

Long, T. R. (n.d.). How Government Solved the Health Care Crisis, www.freenation.org/a/f1213.html (accessed: 22.10.2014).

Marmor, T., & Oberlander, J. (2016). Medicare at 50, In I. G. Cohen et al. (Ed.), *The Oxford Handbook of U.S. Health Law*, Oxford University Press, pp. 742–764.

McGuff, D. & Murphy, R. P. (2015). *The Primal Prescription*. Primal Blueprint Publishing.

Perry, M. J. (2017). If cosmetic surgery has a working market, why can't medical care, www.fee.org/articles/if-cosmetic-surgery-has-a-working-market-why-can-t-medical-care/ (accessed: 24.10.2024).

Pettegrew, L. S., Vance, C. A. (2013). The High Cost of "Free", www.mises.org/library/high-cost-free (accessed: 22.10.2024).

Robbins, G., Robbins, A., Goodman, J. C. (1993). *How are your health care system works*. National Center for Policy Analysis.

Starr, P. (1982). *The Social Transformation of American Medicine*, Basic Books.

Steinreich, D. (2004). Real Medical Freedom, www.mises.org/library/real-medical-freedom (accessed: 22.10.2024).

4 Medicare and Medicaid in the 21st Century

Medicare

In 2018, more than 60 million beneficiaries (more than 18% of the U.S. population) used Medicare, up from 19 million in 1966 (about 9.5% of the population) (CMS, n.d.). During this time, the scope of services provided expanded, and the rules for paying suppliers also changed. However, the cost of funding this programme has been steadily increasing since its inception. In 2008, Medicare spending was $462 billion, and 10 years later it accounted for $731 billion, an increase of 58% (the inflation rate at that time was about 16%). Detailed information is shown in Figure 4.1.

The projected average annual increase in expenditure between 2018 and 2028 is estimated at 7.9%. It is higher than in the years 2010–2018, which averaged 4.4% per year, which is the result of, among other things, budget changes or the influx of younger and healthier beneficiaries generating lower costs, which had an impact on the decrease in the growth rate of expenditure in previous years (Cubansky, Neuman, & Freed, 2019). In turn, according to estimates by the Congressional Budget Office (CBO), total Medicare spending will double from $765 billion in 2019 to $1,552 billion in 2029 (an increase of 103%). The situation is similar when it comes to net spending,[1] which is estimated to increase from $630 billion to $1,278 billion in 2029 (Figure 4.2) (CBO, 2019b).

The CBO also projects that Medicare net spending alone will increase from 3% of GDP in 2019 to 6% of GDP in 2049 (CBO, 2019a). The share of the general fund as a source of funding for the programme will also increase, and the share of Medicare payroll taxes will decrease, as shown in Figure 4.3.

In fact, however, the share of payroll taxes will be smaller than reported. Surplus funds allocated to finance Part A go to the Medicare Trust Fund (The Hospital Insurance Trust Fund). These surpluses are a *reserve* from which future benefits are to be financed if expenses exceed revenues from payroll tax and other sources. However, the assets held in the trust fund are used to purchase Treasury bonds, which the Treasury

DOI: 10.4324/9781003588108-5

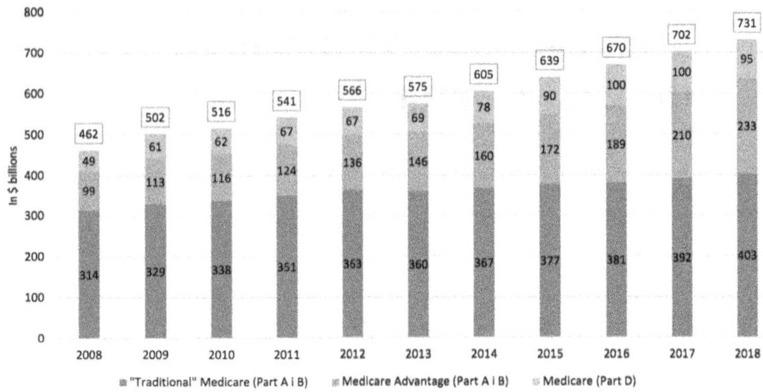

Figure 4.1 Spending on Medicare Parts in 2008–2018.

Source: Own study based on: Cubansky, Neuman, & Freed, 2019.

Note: Medicare (Part D) covers both stand-alone plans and those with Medicare Advantage.

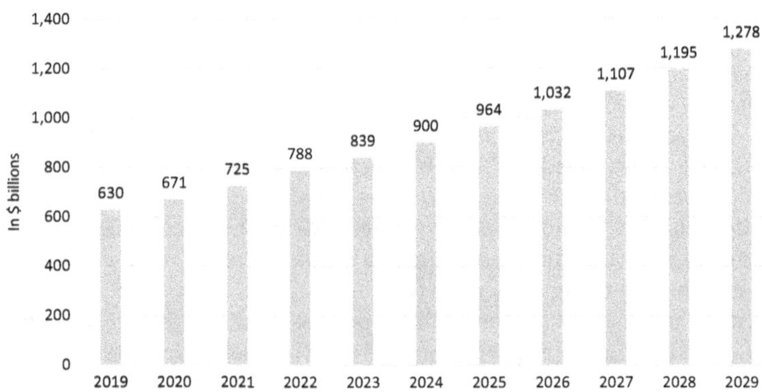

Figure 4.2 Future (projected) net spending on the Medicare programme in 2019–2029.

Source: Own study based on: CBO, 2019b.

Department will repay with future taxes or loans. These funds are immediately spent by the government. Despite what is suggested in official reports, this fund does not have its own resources which had been previously invested in productive ventures. For instance, at the end of 2016, the assets of the Part A trust fund amounted to $199 billion, which is also the total amount of liabilities of the Treasury Department. In turn, revenues for 2017 were $299 billion and expenditures amounted to $297 billion, bringing Medicare's assets to about $202 billion (Tax Policy Center, n.d.).

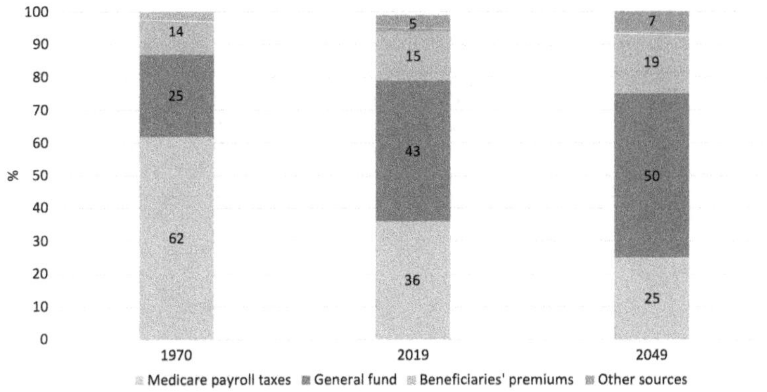

Figure 4.3 Change in Medicare funding sources in selected years.

Source: Own study based on: Peter G. Peterson Foundation (2019).

Note: Other sources include income from the taxation of social security benefits, which are used to finance the cost of Medicare hospital insurance, medication fees, and state transfers. Individual sums may not add up to 100% due to rounding.

Therefore, if the expenditure on Part A exceeds the revenues in the following year, funds from the trust fund will be involved, coming in fact from additional taxes or loans. Thus, taxpayers pay twice. According to 2019 estimates, Part A's assets will be completely depleted in 2026, 2 years from now, which is an indicator of the financial stability of the Medicare programme (Cubansky, Neuman & Freed, 2019). Such calculations, however, are not so important because, as already mentioned, these assets are only accounting entries that tell how much the government borrows to itself at the expense of the taxpayers.

In the case of SMI (Medicare Parts B and D), it is assumed that any shortfall in funds will be covered by additional tax revenue. The main factors behind the growing Medicare spending include the transition of the generation of baby boomers (people born between 1946 and 1964) to retirement (the period from 2011 to 2029) and increasing life expectancy. This leads to a situation in which the ratio of employed people to beneficiaries of social programmes is constantly decreasing; in 1965 it was 4 (4 employees per 1 beneficiary), in 2015 it was 2.8, and in 2035 it will be 2.2, which will increase the burden on taxpayers (Table 4.1) (Social Security Administration, 2018).

However, demographic changes themselves are not a problem. Perceiving them as a problem is a result of flawed solutions adopted in social insurance, where there are no previously accumulated or multiplied savings, and the financing of the current needs of people leaving the labour market comes from people who remain in it.

Table 4.1 Number of insured employees and beneficiaries covered by specific insurance/social programmes in the selected years

Year	*Number of insured employees per one beneficiary of insurance/ social programmes (OASDI)*[a]	*Number of beneficiaries of insurance/social programmes (OASDI)*[a] *per 100 insured employees*
1965	4,0	25
1970	3,7	27
1975	3,2	31
1980	3,2	31
1985	3,3	30
1990	3,4	30
1995	3,3	31
2000	3,4	29
2005	3,3	30
2010	2,9	34
2015	2,8	35
2020	2,7	37
2025	2,5	40
2030	2,3	43
2035	2,2	46
2040	2,2	46
2045	2,2	46
2055	2,2	46
2065	2,1	48
2075	2,1	49
2085	2,1	48
2095	2,0	49

Source: Own study based on: Social Security Administration, 2018.

Note

[a] OASDI – Old Age, Survivors and Disability Insurance; Beneficiaries of OASDI include retirees, orphaned spouses and their children, and workers with disabilities.

Characteristics and costs of Medicaid

The Medicaid programme is also generating increasingly higher costs. In 2014, more than 80 million Americans (25% of the population) benefited from it, with children being the largest group (43% of beneficiaries). However, the largest amount of funding (40%) is allocated to people with disabilities, who account for 14% of the programme's beneficiaries (Figure 4.4).

Medicaid is a federal-state programme that provides funding for medical services to select groups of beneficiaries who are eligible for support. Some of the funding comes from federal sources. This contribution is called Federal Medical Assistance Percentage (FMAP) and is determined by comparing the state's *per capita* income to the national average. Lower-income states receive more federal funding, the minimum contribution of which cannot be less than 50%. In 2017, the federal government covered about 60% of the total cost of Medicaid (Rudowitz, Orgera & Hinton, 2019).

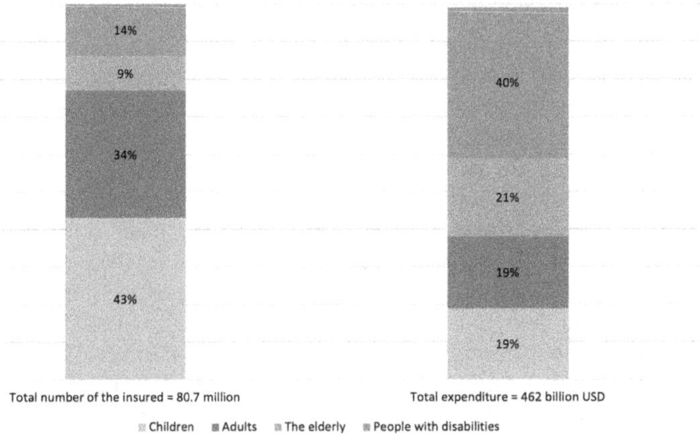

Figure 4.4 Structure of the insured and expenditure for individual groups of Medicaid beneficiaries in 2014.

Source: Own study based on: Rudowitz, Orgera & Hinton, 2019.

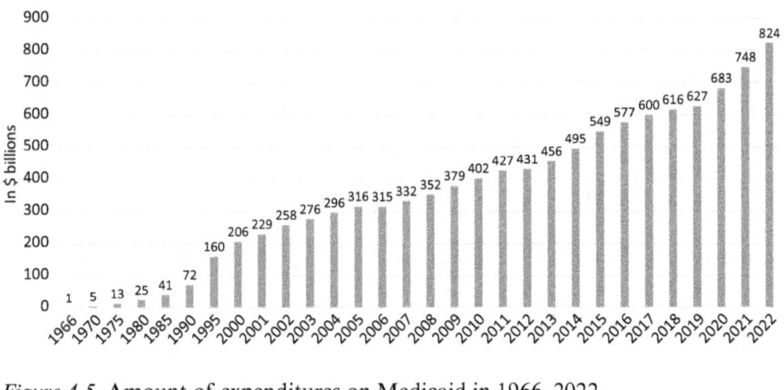

Figure 4.5 Amount of expenditures on Medicaid in 1966–2022.

Source: Own study based on: Statista (n.d.-a), Statista (n.d.-b).

Expenditure on the programme has been steadily increasing, partly due to the expansion of its scope. In 1997, the Children's Health Insurance Program (CHIP), providing medical funding for families with children who cannot afford to self-finance medical care was incorporated into Medicaid. In turn, ObamaCare reform expanded eligible groups to include uninsured adults under age 65 whose income is equal to or lower than 138% of the Federal Poverty Level (FPL). Medicaid spending in 2017 was $600 billion, up from $456 billion in 2013 and $351.9 billion in 2008, which constitutes an increase of about 71%. In subsequent years, spending continues to rise (Figure 4.5).

Medicaid and the fight against poverty

The increasing spending and the number of beneficiaries are continuously increasing their dependence on public health programmes and crowding out charitable institutions. Prior to the introduction of Medicaid and Medicare (and other welfare transfers introduced under President Lyndon Johnson), both the poverty rate and the number of poor people were steadily declining, but this decline was slowed by the increasing amount of money allocated to social transfers, including Medicaid. For instance, the poverty rate fell from around 22% in 1960 to 15% in 1965 and to around 12% in 1969 (11.8% in 2018). The same was true of the number of poor people, which fell from about 40 million in 1960 to about 28 million in 1965 and below 25 million in 1969 (in 2018, the number of poor people was estimated at 38.1 million) (Semega et al., 2019, p. 12). Paradoxically, social programmes that are supposed to help the poor mean that to continue receiving benefits, they must stay poor. The more generous the benefits, the more difficult it is for their beneficiaries to return to the labour market and regain their independence. As Robert Rector (2000, pp. 293–294) points out:

> The welfare system that has existed for the past thirty years may best be conceptualized as a system that offered each single mother with two children a "paycheck" of combined benefits worth an average of between $8,500 and $15,000, depending on the state. The mother had a contract with the government. She would continue to receive her "paycheck" as long as she fulfilled two conditions: 1. She must not work. 2. She must not marry an employed male.

Moreover, as Loyd S. Pettegrew and Carol A. Vance argue (2013), citing data cited by economist Nicholas Eberstadt:

> The political allure of free is so strong that an alarming number of people choose to become wards of the entitlement/welfare state rather than captain their own destiny. Economist Nicholas Eberstadt of the American Enterprise Institute believes that Americans have become a nation of takers, threatening the self-reliance that has long characterized our national psyche. Eberstadt (2012, p. 4) presents data showing that entitlement payments to Americans, since 1960, have risen annually by 9.5 percent. He argues that over the past 50 years the ever-increasing array of transfer payments to Americans have risen 727 percent. In 2010 such payments alone totalled $2.3 trillion with Social Security (for old age and disability) accounting for 31 percent, Medicare 24 percent, Medicaid 18 percent, Income Maintenance 12 percent, other giveaways (free cell-phones, support for a broken

> education system, housing, the arts, etc.) 8 percent, and Unemployment Insurance 6 percent (Eberstadt 2012, C1-2). This has resulted in 49 percent of American households receiving one or more government transfer benefits (Eberstadt 2012); this amounts to 18 percent of all personal income and a burden of $7,400 for every American.[2]

Programmes such as Medicaid compete with charitable institutions which still play an important role in the USA. Despite rising taxes and premiums funding various government programmes, the resources available to American charities are also increasing. For instance, 2017 was a record year for funds raised voluntarily, which amounted to $410 billion compared to $389 billion raised in 2016. It is also impressive that most of the funds raised (70%) come from individual donors. The purposes for which the funds are allocated are very diverse. Most of the funds are donated to religious purposes (31%), educational ones (14%) or personal services (12%). About 9% of the funds are directly transferred to health organizations, however, it does not mean that it is a small amount (Giving USA, 2018).

The development of charitable institutions[3] is a testament to the preservation of the old traditions and values of the American people, despite the growth of many governmental social programmes. The increase in their popularity is a sign of the growing demand for this type of service, which also gives hope for a gradual return to the decentralized and voluntary social safety net that was functioning well in the USA at the turn of the 19th and 20th centuries (Steinreich, 2014, p. 250).

This can be observed, for example, in the World Giving Index (WGI) report devoted to the study of charity in individual countries and published by the Charities Aid Foundation. The report is also based on Gallup research. Respondents are asked to answer three short questions: In the past month, did you: 1) help a stranger or someone you don't know; 2) donate money to charity; 3) dedicate your time to volunteering with a charity? An arithmetic mean is then drawn from the percentage of these three responses (as a percentage). The latest edition of the report – from 2019 – contains aggregate research conducted in the previous 10 years (2009–2018) covering about 1.3 million people. The research shows that the USA is the most charitable country in the world with a score of 58.3%. Of these, 72% of Americans surveyed helped a stranger, 61% donated to charity, and 42% were involved in charitable institutions. Myanmar (Burma) came second (57.6%) and New Zealand third (56.6%) (Charities Aid Foundation, 2019). An example of such an institution is Liberty HealthShare, a religious community that operates as a mutual aid society but is not an insurer. Such institutions are exempt from ObamaCare's requirements for private insurers and offer their members an alternative form of financing access to medical services. Members make a specific monthly contribution (there are three options to choose from) tailored to the current medical needs of the group. A large and geographically diverse community is committed to supporting each other when they make their first out-of-pocket expenses. Any supporter can easily see where their donated funds are going. Voluntary contributions help to create high ethical standards or responsibility for oneself and for others. Thanks to transparent rules and effective solutions, new members join the organization, and the communities themselves develop (followers of other religions can also join such a community).

It is also important that a sick person, who bears part of the costs,[4] gains motivation to recover from the illness with strong spiritual and financial support from other members.[5] The issue of admitting people who are already ill is also interesting. In the first year, the costs are not covered, but the new member receives funds for lifestyle changes (the so-called health truck), which is due to the knowledge that many health problems are the result of people's previous actions. This is in stark contrast to government insurance, which seeks to cover all costs for the insured, which is a road to nowhere, as it indirectly reinforces their sense of being constantly ill. Institutions such as Liberty HealthShare can cover costs of several million dollars if needed. Importantly, thanks to efficient management and a growing community, they are also able to negotiate preferential rates for their members with suppliers. Currently, there are several larger institutions of this type in the USA and dozens of smaller associations – Liberty HealthShare is the largest of them with over 250,000 members.[6]

By contrast, the Medicaid programme is constantly plagued by the reluctance of some doctors to accept new patients. A 2011 nationwide survey of physicians found that 31% of physicians were reluctant to accept new Medicaid patients. Acceptance rates in different states varied widely. According to a study published by Health Affairs, 69% of physicians were seeing Medicaid patients nationwide, but acceptance status ranged from 40% in New Jersey to 99% in Wyoming (Decker, 2012). As another study found, this is due to low Medicaid reimbursement rates, the administrative burden of Medicaid participation, delays in reimbursement, and patient behaviour. Nearly 70% of physicians surveyed considered Medicaid reimbursement rates to be a bigger problem than commercial insurance reimbursement rates.

In addition, for 65.5% of physicians, the complexity of the case of Medicaid patients was more of an issue than for patients with commercial insurance. Some physicians also stated that the needs of Medicaid patients were more complex and included not only physical health care, but also health behaviour and substance abuse care, as well as social services and transportation. Physicians also pointed out that Medicaid patients often have more complicated lives, which can cause them to require a disproportionately larger amount of time and resources from medical professionals (Long, 2019).

Lower reimbursement rates are due, among other things, to artificially stimulated demand and to state policies to control costs by capping payment rates, controlling prescription drug costs, and implementing reforms to the payment and supply system (Rudowitz, Orgera & Hinton, 2019).

Final remarks

In 2018, Medicare, Medicaid, Children's Health Insurance Program (CHIP) and ObamaCare combined accounted for the largest share (26%) of the federal budget (Cubansky, Neuman & Freed, 2019). According to estimates, in the future expenditure on these programmes will grow much faster than expenditure on social security and will already amount to 9.3% of GDP in 2049 (in 2019 it was 5.2% of GDP), as shown in Figure 4.6.

However, from the perspective of economics, the question of the economic and social costs that accompany these trends is much more important. Forecasts from a few decades ago also pointed to growing spending (both nominal and as a percentage of GDP). Theory and experience have shown that higher expenditures do not necessarily mean a slowdown in their growth rate in the future or better access to medical services.

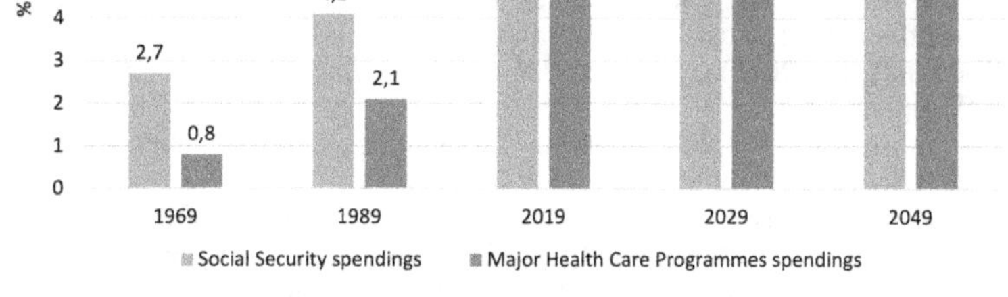

Figure 4.6 Historical and projected share of individual federal government expenditures as a percentage of GDP by year.

Source: Own study based on: CBO, 2019a.

Note: Expenditures on Major Health Care Programmes include: net Medicare expenditures (net of premiums and other compensatory income); Medicaid/CHIP expenditures and expenditures intended to subsidize individuals who purchased their health insurance through Healthcare Insurance Marketplaces.

Notes

1 That is not including the beneficiaries' premiums or other compensation influx.
2 For more, see: Eberstadt, 2012.
3 A list of the largest American charities (including many health organizations) can be found here: Forbes, n.d.
4 The amount of the deductible depends on the selected programme option: in the individual option, the member bears the costs of $1000, in the couples option it is $1750, and the family option amounts to $2000.
5 One of the characteristics of such communities is a very high enthusiasm or optimism in achieving the intended health or spiritual goals.
6 For more, see: Liberty HealthShare, n.d.

References

CBO (2019a). The 2019 Long-Term Budget Outlook, www.cbo.gov/system/files/2019-06/55331-LTBO-2.pdf (accessed: 24.10.2024).

CBO (2019b). Updated Budget Projections: 2019 to 2029, www.cbo.gov/system/files/2019-05/55151-budget_update_0.pdf (accessed: 24.10.2024).

Charities Aid Foundation (2019). The CAF World Giving Index 10th Edition, www.cafonline.org/docs/default-source/about-us-publications/caf_wgi_10th_edition_report_2712a_web_101019.pdf (accessed: 24.10.2024).

CMS (n.d.). Medicare Enrolment – National Trends 1966–2013, www.cms.gov/Research-Statistics-Data-and-Systems/Statistics-Trends-and-Reports/MedicareEnrpts/Downloads/SMI2013.pdf (accessed: 24.10.2024).

Cubansky, J., Neuman, T., & Freed, M. (2019). The Facts on Medicare Spending and Financing, www.kff.org/medicare/issue-brief/the-facts-on-medicare-spending-and-financing/ (accessed: 15.04.2020).

Decker, S. L. (2012). In 2011 Nearly One-Third Of Physicians Said They Would Not Accept New Medicaid Patients, But Rising Fees May Help, www.healthaffairs.org/doi/full/10.1377/hlthaff.2012.0294 (accessed: 24.10.2024).

Eberstadt, N. (2012). *Nation of Takers: America's Entitlement Epidemic*, Templeton Press.

Forbes (n.d.). The 100 Largest U.S. Charities, www.forbes.com/top-charities/list/#tab:rank (accessed: 24.10.2024).

Giving USA (2018). Giving USA 2018: Americans Gave $410.02 Billion to Charity in 2017, Crossing the $400 Billion Mark for the First Time, www.givingusa.org/giving-usa-2018-americans-gave-410-02-billion-to-charity-in-2017-crossing-the-400-billion-mark-for-the-first-time/ (accessed: 27.09.2019).

Liberty HealthShare (n.d.). What Is Shared in Medical Cost Sharing Programs?, www.libertyhealthshare.org/how-it-works (accessed: 24.10.2024).

Long, S. K. (2019). Physicians May Need More Than Higher Reimbursements to Expand Medicaid Participation: Findings from Washington State, www.healthaffairs.org/doi/full/10.1377/hlthaff.2012.1010 (accessed: 24.10.2024).

Peter G. Peterson Foundation (2019). Budget Basics: Medicare, www.pgpf.org/budget-basics/medicare (accessed: 26.09.2019).

Pettegrew, L. S., Vance, C. A. (2013). The High Cost of "Free", www.mises.org/library/high-cost-free (accessed: 22.10.2024).

Rector, R. (2000). Welfare: Broadening the Reform. In S. M. Butler, K. R. Holmes (Ed.), *Issues 2000: The Candidate's Briefing Book*, The Heritage Foundation.

Rudowitz, R., Orgera, K., & Hinton, E. (2019). Medicaid Financing: The Basics, https://files.kff.org/attachment/Issue-Brief-Medicaid-Financing-The-Basics (accessed: 24.10.2024).

Semega, J. et al. (2019). *Income and Poverty in the United States: 2018*. Government Printing Office.

Social Security Administration (2018). The 2018 Annual Report of the Board of Trustees of the Federal Old-Age and Survivors Insurance and Federal Disability Insurance Trust Funds, www.ssa.gov/oact/TR/2018/tr2018.pdf (accessed: 24.10.2024).

Statista (n.d.-a). Total Medicaid expenditure from 1966 to 2019, www.statista.com/statistics/245348/total-medicaid-expenditure-since-1966/ (accessed: 27.09.2019).

Statista (n.d.-b). Total Medicaid expenditure from 1975 to 2022, www.statista.com/statistics/245348/total-medicaid-expenditure-since-1966/ (accessed: 24.10.2024).

Steinreich, D. (2014). 'Book Review: Welfare and Old Age in Europe and North America', *The Quarterly Journal of Austrian Economics 2014*, 18(2): 249–259.

Tax Policy Center (n.d.), What is the Medicare trust fund, and how is it financed?, www.taxpolicycenter.org/briefing-book/what-medicare-trust-fund-and-how-it-financed (accessed: 24.10.2024).

Summary

From the perspective of the Austrian School of Economics, it can be said that the health care system of the USA is part of the so-called hampered economy, where the government interferes in health care by means of orders and prohibitions.

The amount of spending on health care as a share of GDP is much higher in the USA than in other countries and in 2013 (the last year before ObamaCare) it amounted to 16.4% (OECD, 2015, p. 167). To compare, the Netherlands and Switzerland have an 11.1% share of GDP, and the OECD countries average constitutes 8.9% of GDP. In turn, on a per capita basis, it was $8,713 for the USA ($4,197 for public spending and $4,516 for private spending), $6,235 for Switzerland (second in line), and $3,453 for the OECD average (OECD, 2015, p. 165). Although the share of public spending on health care in the United States is slightly lower and in 2013 amounted to less than half, this does not mean that the remaining ('private') part is spent without any state influence. This fact is an interesting field for economic research, as many observers mistakenly believe that the American system is typically market-oriented. However, the market is not only about private entities (e.g., private insurers) but also about far-reaching freedom in insurance business activities.

The increase in insurance premiums has been very burdensome for employees, their families and employers for many years. However, the market is vastly over-regulated which makes it very difficult for private insurers to offer cheaper plans based on risk selection and classification. Unfortunately, but in the USA, insurers are prohibited from offering low-cost health insurance. This is important because in 2014, over 50% of the entire U.S. population was covered by some type of private health insurance. Therefore, it seems important to point out the reasons for this state of affairs.

However, the private health insurance market, despite its problems, is one of the main barriers to the introduction of mandatory government insurance for all Americans. Proponents of this idea must take into account not only the resistance of institutions such as the AMA, which

DOI: 10.4324/9781003588108-6

have already opposed such plans in the past, but also the obstacle of the health insurance market, including self-financing plans. A single-payer system would have to severely restrict this market, which would mean depriving workers of access to medical services, tax benefits, etc. Such reasoning also leads to the conclusion that any intervention that destabilizes this market is another step (consciously or not) on the way to the introduction of this system.

An economic approach is essential to a proper understanding of the health care problems of the USA (and any other country) because economics is the science of meeting the needs of people in a world of shortages and constraints – including those related to medical goods and services. If the analyses and warnings of economists are not considered, even the greatest achievements of medicine or the most effective management will not solve the existing problems. Ignoring the laws of economics has its consequences, and this study should also be treated as a warning against such attitudes.

The key interventions are shown in Tables 5.1 and 5.2 which show that the consequences of interventionism do not have to be immediate but, over time, even mild interventions can have serious consequences in the future. This applies to both private and government health insurance.

Table 5.1 Key interventions in the health insurance market and their effects

Year/period	*Interventions*
1930s	Introduction of tax preferences for Blue Cross/Blue Shield plans in exchange for the use of community rating in the calculation of premiums.
Mid 1940s	Introduction of tax preferences for employee health insurance as one of the effects of price and wage controls during World War II.
1944	The antitrust regulations related to the Sherman Act are coming into force for the health insurance market.
1945	The McCarran–Ferguson Act is passed, thanks to which insurance companies do not have to comply with the regulations contained in the Sherman Act.
From 1950s	However, the McCarran–Ferguson Act meant that states were given the power to protect customers from the monopolistic practices of insurers. This resulted in a significant interference in the prices and scope of health insurance. From the second half of the 20th century, there is a significant increase in state regulations, which contributes to the rise of insurance prices.
1974	Enactment of the Employee Retirement Security Act (ERISA) which allows employers to act as an "insurer" by creating their own health plans (the so-called self-financing).

(*Continued*)

Table 5.1 (Continued)

Year/period	*Interventions*
1980s and 1990s	Problems with rising insurance costs are prompting insurers to introduce plans based on *managed care* to optimize expenses, which is only partially successful.
Early 21st century	At the beginning of the 21st century, the rate of premium growth continues to accelerate, which is increasingly prompting employers to look for alternatives to health insurance in the form of self-financing plans which now cover more than half of all employees. Employers are also more willing to use the services of retail chains or medical tourism, i.e., services not financed by insurance.
From 2005/2006	Rising insurance costs contribute to an increase in direct costs incurred by employees, such as deductibles.
From 2010	Faced with problems with prices inflated by suppliers, insurers are starting to look for alternative sources of revenue. Such actions result in an increase in the share of their revenues from technology services and from servicing the government Medicare and Medicaid insurance. The insurance offer of insurers is becoming more and more similar to government programmes.
2013/2014	New regulations for insurers related to the ObamaCare regulations.

Source: Own study.

Table 5.2 Key interventions in the area of government health programmes and their effects

Year/period	*Interventions*
1930s	New Blue Cross/Blue Shield health plans are being developed as an alternative to health insurance. Plans of this type are gaining approval from doctors and AMAs. Additional benefits include tax exemptions in exchange for the use of unified risk assessment criteria (community rating).
1965	As a result of the aeging of their insured/members, The Blues incur higher and higher costs and lose the competition with insurers that do not use community ratings. There is growing pressure to relieve the financial burden on these institutions by creating government insurance covering the elderly (Medicare) and poorer members of society (Medicaid).
Until 1983	Medicare finances access to medical services on a cost-plus basis, which means that Medicare covers all costs for services provided by providers. This leads to overpricing by providers (e.g., hospitals) and a significant increase in Medicare spending.
From 1983	A new payment system – DRG – is introduced. As a result of limited payments from Medicare, providers begin to price their services to insurers, which leads to higher premiums. Over time, insurers also take measures to reduce payments to hospitals and develop, e.g., outpatient care.

(*Continued*)

Table 5.2 (Continued)

Year/period	*Interventions*
Early 1990s	There are new regulations - Evaluation and Management (E&M) – with a similar goal to DRG, but this time covering outpatient care. This leads to a significant increase in the number of administrative employees and even greater bureaucratization of the system, which has a negative impact on the quality of services provided by doctors.
21st century	The expansion of Medicare coverage means that this programme covers more and more Americans and becomes more and more expensive. Between 2008 and 2018, total spending on this programme increased by 58%, while the inflation rate increased by 16%.
21st century	According to CBO estimates, the projected net spending on Medicare in 2029 will amount to almost $1,300 billion. In 2019, they amounted to $630 billion.
21st century	The costs and scope of the Medicaid programme are also increasing. In 2017, spending on this programme amounted to $600 billion, while in 2008 it was $352 billion. In 2014, this programme covered 25% of the U.S. population.
2011	A nationwide survey found that 31% of physicians were unwilling to admit new Medicaid patients, partly due to low reimbursement rates and complex medical cases requiring more time.
2049	According to CBO estimates, the share of federal spending on major health care programmes in 2049 will amount to 9.3% of GDP. In 2019, it was 5.2%, and in 1989 it was 2.1%.

Source: Own study.

Reference

OECD (2015). *Health at a Glance 2015: OECD Indicators*. OECD Publishing.

Index

Pages in *italics* refer to figures and pages in **bold** refer to tables.

For Product Safety Concerns and Information please contact our EU representative GPSR@taylorandfrancis.com
Taylor & Francis Verlag GmbH, Kaufingerstraße 24, 80331 München, Germany

www.ingramcontent.com/pod-product-compliance
Lightning Source LLC
LaVergne TN
LVHW021113300926
849160LV00009B/725
9781032961248